WRITING *and the*
SPIRITUAL LIFE

Finding Your Voice by Looking Within

Patrice Vecchione

Contemporary Books

Chicago New York San Francisco Lisbon London Madrid Mexico City
Milan New Delhi San Juan Seoul Singapore Sydney Toronto

Library of Congress Cataloging-in-Publication Data

Vecchione, Patrice.
   Writing and the spiritual life : finding your voice by looking within /
Patrice Vecchione.
       p.   cm.
   Includes biographical references.
   ISBN 0-8092-2497-6
   1. Spiritual journals—Authorship.   2. Spiritual life.   I. Title.

BL628.5 .V43   2001
808'.02—dc21   00-45176

Contemporary Books

A Division of The McGraw·Hill Companies

1 2 3 4 5 6 7 8 9 0   AGM/AGM   0 9 8 7 6 5 4 3 2 1

ISBN 0-8092-2497-6

This book was set in Centaur MT
Printed and bound by Quebecor Martinsburg

Cover design by Jeanette Wojtyla

McGraw-Hill books are available at special quantity discounts to use as premiums
and sales promotions, or for use in corporate training programs. For more
information, please write to the Director of Special Sales, Professional Publishing,
McGraw-Hill, Two Penn Plaza, New York, NY 10121-2298. Or contact your local
bookstore.

Literary credits appear on page 219, which should be considered an extension of
this copyright page.

This book is printed on acid-free paper.

To Michael Stark,
No matter the ocean,
shore

And to Marion Silverbear,
First reader, guardian angel,
friend

CONTENTS

ACKNOWLEDGMENTS

For their generous attention to this book—questions and answers, guidance and tenderness—many thanks to Alison Bermond (for sorting through the pieces, particularly the ones underneath), Janet Greenberg (queen of section headings and longtime friend), and Don Rothman (our lunches at Gabriella's). My love is yours.

I'm grateful to my mother, Peggy Vecchione, who began the love of words and where they can take us in me, and for her belief which helped me to locate mine. For noticing light and color, and for saying what he saw, gratitude to my father, Nick Vecchione.

To Wendy Traber and Gina Van Horn, my deepest thanks for your abiding friendship.

For reading, conversation, faith, and notes in the margins, many thanks to Diane Atchison, Nanda Currant, Jenny D'Angelo, Jasmin Gerer, David Harrington, Carl Larkin, Susan Lyon, Sandi Miller, Jerilyn Munyon, Sharman Murphy, Nancy Norris (all those years), Janis O'Driscoll, Sarah Rabkin, Helen Resneck, Barbara Stark, and Roy Stark.

To Jorge Chino, for your help with translating the beehive poem, thank you.

To David Stocker, thanks for your computer wizardry that saved the day.

Gratitude to Wendy Middleton for her hands-on support, helping me to be at home in my body.

To my agent Charlotte Raymond, infinite thanks for your support of this book. I can't imagine it without you.

Heartfelt thanks to my editor Matthew Carnicelli, and that particular March message which remains on my telephone answering machine for periodic playback. Many thanks to project editor Caroline McCoy for her guidance. Thank you also to publicist Brigid Brown.

Writers Marvin Bell, Joseph Bruchac, Mary Gordon, Joy Harjo, Brenda Hillman, Maurice Kenny, Madeleine L'Engle, Philip Levine, Morton Marcus, Carole Maso, Deena Metzger, Pat Mora, Carol Muske-Dukes, Naomi Shihab Nye, Elizabeth Spires, Mary Swander, and Helena Maria Viramontes responded with insight, wisdom, and some necessary humor to my questions about the connections between writing and spirituality.

Thank you to my students—participants in the weekend workshops and teachers' inservices, and the monthly women's writing group—including Susan Ford, Darrie Ganzhorn, Linda Holiday, Kathryn Kefauver, Susan Keniston, Lisa Livingston, Laurie Talcott, Ariel Thiermann, Barbara Warsavage, Susan Watrous, and those who come to the Santa Cruz County Public Library to write during the Poetry by the Bay workshops.

For research assistance, many thanks to the reference librarians at the Monterey Public Library, Victor H. Bausch, Tamara Hennessy, Doug Holtzman, and Steve Parker.

To Wade Hall and Harry Gurnee at Spokeman Bicycles, and the people at Kestrel, and to Charlie Verutti and Matt Ryan, for my two-wheeled, winged machine, miles of thanks.

INTRODUCTION

To me writing is life, it is my way of being most fully alive.

Ursula Le Guin

When a writer sits down at her desk, she initiates a journey that will lead her to language and personal transformation. By turning to a clean sheet of paper and picking up a pen, she begins to give form to something nebulous within. It's an attempt to connect the invisible to the visible, to turn it into words. The world of spirit and daily life—that of the mind, the soul, and the body—come together when the writer dips into the subconscious to clarify, determine, and steady. Writing can rescue us from emptiness. The paper is blank. And onto this blank canvas, a landscape of language will make hills and valleys and curves in the road. How the paper becomes filled with language, how the writer chooses one particular word to follow another, is mysterious. Through writing and staying in tune to the calling of the work, the words are found and, each upon the next, build what has to be said. Gaston Bachelard, in *The Poetics of Reverie*, said, "The blank page gives us the right to dream." We dream our way into the telling.

In articles, interviews, and informal conversations, writers discuss the quality of surprise and mystery inherent in the act of writing—

be it story, poem, or essay—and that the experience is beyond the ordinary, beyond the predictability of logic. Even when one has a pretty clear idea of what one wants to say, the act of writing itself influences both content and style. The way is not a straight line; it's unplanned, bumpy, and at times jagged. Writing can be an unlit walk through a dark place. No flashlight here or street lamp, though sometimes there's the confidence of a pale moon. The absence of illumination doesn't necessarily imply the ominous, but rather an experience veiled in enigma. And yet a suggestion of fear may be present, often manifested as excitement or doubt and accompanied by questions such as, "If I don't know exactly what I have to say, might it be what I've been told never to speak? And, if I speak that something, then what?" These unavoidable questions are an essential part of the risk of writing, the experience of weaving the known and the unknown, what seems possible and what seems impossible to say. The writer cuts across what's acceptable, breaks into the underworld with its molten rock and chaos, and through sorting, being attentive, and spending time in the spiritual practice of writing, works her way back up to the light.

As long as there is nothing on the page, one may feel a lack, nothing, with its implication of emptiness, nowhere, no one—abandonment and, ultimately, the fear of death. The writer moves up to this edge and backs away from it. The passion for what there is to say carries him on. Absence, by its nature, also connotes opportunity, what's yet to come. From out of nothing, anything can spring. This is the act of creation. All creation is about making something from nothing. The art is your other, the loved one. You taste this craving at the back of your throat like pollen. It can be dizzying, this call toward the words' unveiling. To move toward the crystallization of thought, awareness, and emotion is joyous.

Writing can serve many functions. An affair of the heart can begin with the written word. We may be summoned, freed, or imprisoned through what's written down. We use writing to promise, to lie and to tell the truth, to hide and to be found. Writing starts revolutions and helps us make peace. It can be a form of witness, a way to chronicle both justice and injustice. It can be used for matters lofty or mundane. The written word can change our fortunes.

When we use writing to make art, we dive into deep water. Our writing becomes the talisman, proof of where we've been and what we've encountered. Camile Paglia wrote, "At the root of our compulsion to create art is the need to establish some calm point within life's turbulent flow." Writing can be an anchor in our lives. We transition from the clean page to the dizzying rush of word upon word to the saying said and the calm point that comes after the spirit has manifested itself in language. The paper holds the words; they are secure and steady there. We become steady as well. For the time being, mystery has unveiled itself.

THE SPIRITUAL PATH OF WRITING

The poet Joy Harjo writes, "Spirituality is the sacred relationship with the creative force that has called us and all universes into being. . . . I am humble before this shimmering, creative force and I know that I am a fool before it." Writing can be a way we connect with the spiritual forces that support our lives, a way to be in the presence of holiness and to honor the mystery of life and creation. This book will help you connect with your inborn creativity, develop an intimate relationship with it, and recognize the spiritual nature of your inner self. You can take the vague longing for a spiritual life and transform it into an active and satisfying practice that constitutes a genuine and personal path. To write spiritually is to engage in a search for authentic language. You'll find your truth by writing your way to it. Through writing, you may discover answers to essential questions like, "How do I find peace?" and "Where is the presence of God in my life?" Writing can provide you with an inspired way to interact with the sacred realms as well as to find meaning in daily life. Here, you'll discover how writing can be, as Erica Jong says, "My meditation, my medicine, my prayer, my solace."

You know more than you know you know. Everyone does. We each have years of experience behind us, as well as the details of this particular day. If you try to recall all of your life in one sitting, you will either sit for years or jump at the thought of it, as there is obviously more than the mind can hone in on all at once. There is the way an event from when you were eight somehow coincides with something that happened yesterday. Links between various experiences exist pre-verbally and seemingly illogically.

To be alive is not primarily a linear experience. It's a mix of dreaming and running to the store for a quart of milk. Our lives have depth, in part, because we can't make sense of everything. Life doesn't make sense; it's more complicated than our linear way of knowing. Mystery and spirit run through our days like rivers and sustain us. Life is a blend of possibility and impossibility; to write well, the writer must convey the complex sense of what it means to be alive at a given moment. The writer speaks the multilayered complexity of what it is to be human—to fail and to succeed, to be diminished and raised up. The writer must capture nuance and delicacy, roughness and the broken edge. That can't be done from the outside, only from within.

Writing as a spiritual practice helps us accept that the unexpected ideas and images that come together will resonate with truth. By writing in a way that accepts and integrates our many ways of knowing, we allow secrets and connections to come out on the page. By trusting what isn't obvious and what doesn't make sense, we are able to return to and write about what we thought we had forgotten, what we deeply long to say. We encounter the "aha," a revelation that clarifies, that makes the bridge and demonstrates that one seemingly unconnected thing is actually perfectly paired with another. And congruency is reached once again. From chaos comes clarity. It was there all along. You just couldn't see it. To come to clarity, you have to enter the chaos. Dive in or enter inch by inch. Confusion is not a bad thing. The writer Pat Mora said, "What is our practice? Struggling with writing is a kind of spiritual practice." Just as with any spiritual or political path, to be called to it doesn't mean the way will be clear. Welcome the difficult parts, as they will lead you to a depth you could arrive at no other way.

Once the words have found each other and you have found your soul in them, your perceptions change. You no longer rely solely on old ways of knowing and perceiving but are riveted by this new way that accepts and welcomes, with grace, the unsolved questions and the complete mystery of being alive. New work continues to be generated as a result of this transformation. This change will extend beyond the page and influence your daily life. There'll be more soulfulness and spirit there.

This larger awareness is part of the realm of the sacred, and for many writers, it is an essential aspect of their spiritual lives. The experience of being engaged in writing is a kind of prayer. One has an elevated awareness that lets one write deeply, with a freshness that is free of predictability and clichés. The writer begins to listen, may feel lightheaded, and may even notice a change in his breathing pattern. His awareness of the sensory details of the surrounding room diminishes. His sense of time shifts—has an hour gone by or only a minute? And while in this altered state, he writes past himself. Ideas come together like new lovers. To proceed from here, the writer must work to ensure that he is not so far into the ecstasy of the act of *saying* that he's left all potential readers behind. But that can't be considered until there's material to work with. The writer must risk failing and being misunderstood, because if he doesn't have faith in the invisible saying, language will stay at an unreachable distance. The writing won't be true to the writer's potential. And what is written will lack soul and spirit; it will be a dry thing with its edges yellowing and curling under.

Writers talk about how a poem or story writes itself, how it already exists and they see that their job is to find it—work it, yes, but first find it. When a writer accepts that the poem or story is of the world of soul and spirit, past the reach of everyday thinking, then that writer experiences a sense of trust in the creative process. Trust and faith and practice are what spiritual writing lives are built on.

This search for language is similar to the search for God. In both cases one is reaching for what is just beyond one's view, for that which cannot be verified. William Carlos Williams once said that "only the imagination is real," but the imagination is forever fickle, unreliable. Faith is what gives it teeth. Faith, luck, and persistence, returning day after day to the temple door and praying for admittance. In the search for God, we are buoyed by belief and need. Experiencing the invisible in one form allows us to trust it in another form.

Ultimately, both the longing for God and the longing for poetry and story are never satisfied. The need for them is never completely sated. It's like aching for a parent who died before you were born. When writing, you feel as though you have caught it—the impulse, the imagination, the saying has been said for the moment—only to realize you haven't quite said it all. The words are almost complete, but there is more to say. How to say it better?

Some say each of us has only one story to tell, and we try but never completely tell this story, and this is what motivates the work. The one story cannot ever, at one time, in one poem or in one book, be completed. No one text can hold it. And it isn't stagnant but grows as we do. This elusive quality of writing keeps many writers' pencils sharp. The next story will be closer; it will hold the vapor. And God will be found. We'll meet Him in the next poem. If mystery is the foundation of being, then language and spiritual belief are two ways of responding to what cannot be explained.

Many of us weren't raised to regard this inward-searching aspect of the self that is not located primarily in the physical world but is quiet, reverent, and questing. It's not about the bottom line or the net result or one's gross income. What a spiritual writing practice will do is reacquaint writers with the deeper meaning in their lives. It will give answers and then more questions. It will accompany them, this dialogue with the self. It provides a foundation from which to move outward into the world of action. Writing as spiritual practice is prayer and meditation and language crafting all at once.

In American culture, having a calling is at once admired and shunned. Human nuance and depth seem too ephemeral to be embraced, too outside the realm of the external life. The idea of having a spiritual or literary calling is appealing if it's like a badge that we can pin on and remove at will. But to be bound by a calling isn't just romance, glitz, and promise. Culturally, we may love the notion of a calling but not the hard, messy work, complete with failures. The idea that a calling is beyond rational thinking isn't a comforting thought for those who are primarily linearly minded. A calling isn't something you can bank on, and it offers no guarantees. It might take you where you never wanted to go.

Both spiritual seekers and artists are considered to have callings, which they answer through their religious practice or their artistic endeavors. To respond to the calling is to accept an invitation. Yet you can't completely know to what you are being invited—a gala event or a kidnapping. Both, really! When you're driven to write, the writing is writing you, and it's like being taken—you are not where you were before or where you will be once you close your notebook. There is nothing better than feeling the words come on their own—no prodding, pleading, or negotiating. You feel your way into knowing.

The best part isn't when the poem or story makes it to publication, though of course there is significant and valuable reward in that. I find the best part is in the midst of the first draft, maybe when you know you're two-thirds of the way through, and you find the right words coming to the page, no impostors. The poet Rainer Maria Rilke speaks to this in the opening of his poem "Moving Forward": "The deep parts of my life pour onward, as if the river shores were opening out." You're in love and no one else is there. The words may, and probably will, disappoint you another time, but not now, for now you and your words belong to each other.

There is no promise that will automatically be fulfilled by writing. And there may be masters less difficult to follow. The act of writing doesn't necessarily become easy through years of practice. What many writers have found is, the way begets the way: writing compels them to write. After a time of writing, one's trust in the process becomes more secure. The distance between the writer and the words decreases. Yet, at times, this isn't true. When there is something big attempting to be said, the words may seem hidden. I have noticed that after particularly long and difficult fallow times, my new work has a different cast to it—apparent in the content of the material, the style, the form, or the voice. After a time, the writer discovers what hinders her creativity, what will foster it, and how to move toward that. When she welcomes the spiritual into writing, the base from which she works broadens. It's like the ground on which she stands is wider and firmer. In the realm of the sacred, the writer is held by more than individual ego.

"For the Notebook"

Each chapter closes with a section titled "For the Notebook," which consists of one or more suggestions for writing. The content is based on the subjects in the chapter and is designed to help you carry the material into your inner life, your writing life. These sections are not meant as assignments but as inspiration. And if a particular exercise doesn't light your fire, leave it be and go to another, or respond to what's come up for you in the chapter by writing what you will. You may wish to return to some of the exercises later. There may be those that strike you and you want to respond to them again. We're never the same; notice how you're called to write something entirely different about a topic you responded to weeks or months ago. My hope is that you'll interact with this book and that you'll talk back to what you read. I'd like my writing to lead you into conversations with yourself and others—friends, family, colleagues, other writers on the path.

These guided exercises have been written with the individual writer in mind; however, they may be adapted to writing groups. If you are part of, or wish to form, a writer's circle, one member of the group could read the exercise to the others. For the session, that member would serve as facilitator as well as a writer, so that she might support those needing a bit more conversation before beginning to write.

For all your future writing, a notebook will be a fine companion. Whether you choose a loose-leaf binder or a sturdy hardback journal, a tiny fit-in-the-palm-of-your-hand notepad or a large artist's sketchbook, pull it out and begin to make it yours. Sometimes I adorn the inside covers of new notebooks with my current favorite quotations and poems; those words serve as reminders when I open my notebook to write. Or I make collages for the outside covers. Often I'll paste photographs of the natural world or pictures from my travels—actual or imaginary. In any case, the idea is to baptize the book, but not with water! How can you make an anonymous book a home for your words, turn it into a destination for your spirit? What introduction does it need to become a carrier of your heart words?

Many writers keep several books going at once—one for dreams, another for quotes from overheard conversations and best-loved books, one that collects writing project ideas, a daily journal, a back-pocket pad for writing on the run. I like one notebook at a time. More than that and I'd never remember which one was for what and where they all were. Also, I'm drawn to my notebooks as timekeepers; they hold the period of time in which I'm writing in them, so I want all of what I'm influenced by and want to pay attention to in the same spot.

Where are you going to put this book? I keep it in the same corner of my room; then when I want it, it's always there for a quick toss in the backpack on my way to the beach or for my dreams. Nearly every morning, I take my notebook back to bed and write while I'm drinking my first cup of coffee. Even on those mornings I have to be out of the house early, I wake a little sooner so I can capture what needs to be caught before the day catches me.

It is my hope that *Writing and the Spiritual Life* will accompany you on your journey and help you deal with your questions, hopes, and doubts about writing. In these pages, you will find a place to begin your seeking, a way to house your longing for the saying, and a guide to bring you nearer to—and engage in conversation with—your authentic self.

Writing is the only way I know how to pray.

Helena Maria Viramontes

I have simply wanted to show that whenever life seeks
to shelter, protect, cover, or hide itself, the imagination
sympathizes with the being that inhabits
that protected space.

Rainer Maria Rilke

CHAPTER 1

SANCTUARY OF THE SELF

Writing from Home

☙

Perhaps this is the house in which I lived
when neither I, nor earth, existed,
when everything was moon, or stone, or shadow . . .

Pablo Neruda, from Pablo Neruda: Selected Poems

T his book is about where you live. I don't mean physical dwellings, whether you sleep at night in a silver Streamline trailer in a suburban trailer park or in a bungalow at the edge of a wilderness canyon. It's not about the view you have from your kitchen window, the height of your ceilings, whether you have central heating or warm your home with a wood fire.

I'm referring to the place where your truest self resides: in the body but not in the body; the heart but not just the heart; the mind but not limited to the mind. The place you go inside when you're hurt or dreaming. It's where you come from and has been called the "seat of consciousness." The Hindu term for it is *Atman*, the divine, innermost soul that exists in every creature.

When the impossible knocks at your door, it's from this central location within that you answer, that folded, sequestered, resonant place. This is where the long sigh is born. A perpetual hum resounds. Here's the soul's dwelling place, where your greatest knowing begins, where your wisdom comes from. Call it home. You reach out from here and return to this dwelling place. It's where you're most uniquely yourself and simultaneously most like everyone else. You recognize your self and know you are sufficient. This is the residence of your spiritual self.

When you develop a relationship with this aspect of the self through a spiritual writing practice, you can know it better and derive a greater connection to it and to that self within others. You can attain a profound understanding about the self and your sense of soul, God, and the value of living an examined life. By checking in, returning home, and writing from this place, you will strengthen it, steady it, and help it grow. The knowledge and awareness that will come to you from your inner home can give you a base from which to deepen your writing life and, thus, your entire life.

MORE THAN ONE LIFE

We live more than one life at a time. There's the inner life and the outer one, each informing, affecting, and directing the other. My skin responds to rain as a sudden coolness comes over me. The invisible, interior responses to being in the rain are not necessarily the same as what I experience physically. When I'm caught by surprise in the rain, I am reminded of other times that's happened—like that summer day in New York City, running under a movie theater awning to get dry and then deciding to go in and see the film. Both the inner and outer awarenesses come into play in writing, and the two can have a conversation. The philosopher Maurice Merleau-Ponty said, "The body of the painter is the site of 'secret and feverish genesis of things.'" The deeper the practice, the more the seen and the unseen come together to make the work. Some experiences have more inner light focused on them and affect us more deeply, while other events are felt closer to the surface. But it's not only a combination of inner and outer. There are so many ways to live and know our lives.

You might think of life as being lived on more than one plane, like an elevator that can stop at any of a building's many floors. When you press the button for the third floor, the elevator stops there, and you can get out and walk around or continue to another floor. If the intimate, inner self is on the first floor, then the lives we lead that are closest to the self are on the second and third floors, and so on. Or you might consider the image of a wheel. If the self is the wheel's axle, then the parts of one's life are the spokes. The outer rim might be considered the whole world beyond the self—nature, the universe, God. But God also resides at the shaft on which the wheel rotates.

What are the parts that constitute your self? How do you view its aspects? I see an observer and a participant, a questioner and an answerer. There's an awake self and a part who'd rather sleep. One part thrives indoors and wants only comfort; another is made for the wind and tides. The poet Joy Harjo puts it this way, "I know I walk in and out of several worlds every day." What are the worlds you walk in and out of daily? We carry on life in the work-for-money world, which may or may not coincide with our soul world. There's the family life, the social and religious life, and the political life, to whatever degree we participate in them. There are your intimate relationships, the people with whom you communicate on the soul level, which is distinct from a purely social life. There's the life of the body and its workings, which intersects with the soul life but not always. As I move deeper toward my center, I greet the part that cannot separate itself from others' sorrow, the part that knows things before they happen.

The dreamer may be the most awake part of the self, as it's alert to a reality far beyond what's understood by the rational mind. The need for home can be so strong it comes to us in dreams. And it may be in our dream lives that we come closest to it. The dreamer is linked to mystery, a primary aspect of soul life and of good writing.

THE WRITING LIFE

The way a long work is completed is by daily tapping the first imaginative impulses. That's got to be so strong that it never dies in the course of the whole performance.

PAUL HORGAN

Writing this book I feel like a distance runner instead of the sprinter I feel like when I'm writing poems. Some very different things are required of the writer on a long project, including a quality of energy that has to be sustained. The thing I'm most struck by right now is how I'm truly living two distinct lives. One is the loving, social life, and to categorize it as the "outer life" would be to limit its reality. It includes both my inner and outer lives. As does the writing life.

The world of this book is inside me. What I experience on the inside, alone at my desk, affects how I perceive all external life. I'm not who I was before I began this writing. I feel farther away from the outside and closer to the inside.

Because this book is the primary center of my life right now, my daily spiritual practice, there's a way in which nearly everything else is secondary. This cannot be said, entirely, of my closest relationships, though even they are experienced through the filter of this book. Everything I read, think about, live, and dream influences what I write here. This book is where I live. The day-in, day-out writing is my spiritual practice. I've set up camp here. And I'd rather you didn't come find me. Luckily, my friends are kind and give me lots of slack. I don't go to movies because then the images would enter into my inner world. I've become a sponge. I don't want to entertain much. Some days, after lots of writing, I find talking to anyone other than my husband, Michael, difficult. I feel verbally monosyllabic. My body has become a vessel; it's not the source of this work, merely a conduit for something I've been living for and with, for nearly my whole life.

WHERE DO YOU LIVE?

It is dark inside the body, and wet,
and double-hearted. There are so many ways
to go, and not see, and lose
the feeling of the thread . . .
and never reach the fabled center.

LARISSA SZPORLUK, from "One Thousand Bullfrogs Rejoice"

"So many ways to go, and not see." Within myself, I can bump up against God and still not trust Him. Then it's like being away from the loved one I ache for. I'm far from myself, my soul, my truth. It's the home within, that secure center, I'm longing to return to. Sometimes I can write myself back. I follow the path the words make and return to my inner self. Other times I pray to return. Or I may toss and turn for days, feeling off-kilter. Chapter 8 talks about being away from the central writing self and the words that can come from there.

For as many ways as there are to go and *not* see, there are at least as many ways to go *and* see. And what can we do to not "lose the feeling of the thread"? We can begin to identify our stronghold, the spiritual residence of the self. Where is your "fabled center"? When asked to write about where they lived, two eight-year-old girls, Selena and Amelia, responded by picking up their pencils and dashing off to corners of the room and dropping onto the floor. Selena's poem began: "Where is it? A comfy pillow made of fluffy cotton like a mermaid's purse around a shark's egg, a place where my dreams wander as if they were young. . . ." And her friend Amelia wrote, "My home is inside me. It is a place where orange blossoms float above my head."

The place where I am most at home, the place where my soul resides, feels located in and around my heart and a little below, in my solar plexus. When I am aware of that part of my self, attend to it, and act from it, I am at home. There's a sense that everything I am comes together in that location; all inner roads lead there.

If you were to consider the place where you live to be in your body, where would it be? Where's the seat of your soul? The image of a seat is perfect because it's when we sit down that we stop. The visual artist James Turrell remembers his grandmother telling him that, when sitting in Quaker silence, "You were to go inside and greet the light." That's it! Where is your light, your soul's home, and how do you get inside to find it? My friend Marion writes, "There's only one way to go home, there's only one way to be 'somebody,' only one way to know the truth in the moment. There are thousands, maybe millions, of paths but only one sure route: through the heart, in this moment, to trust. It's the open secret." To trust this heart of yours, take the path that leads you to the words of your inner self; it's the only way to go.

Susan, a musician who's studied poetry with me, wrote this about her sense of home:

Spirit is dynamic and moving; it weaves through the world, and the world weaves through it, as wind and leaves enter one another. So it is with the physical experience of inhabiting a body. It gives me certain powers, but many days I can't say with certainty that there's actually a place in my body where I live. It's paradoxical: without eyes, I don't see a dustless blue sky; without my skin, I don't feel the cold of snow or the heat of sun; without ears, no wind, no chickadee. And yet, when I feel most alive, it seems that I'm not separate from those beings, that I don't live "here" and they, "there." I inhabit them,

and they, me. If I'm living anywhere, it's in gratitude—to be alive
in this body, opening myself to the beings around me and knowing that I am like them, an embodiment of the beauty of the
unseen world.

The divisions between self and other, between self and world, slip,
and there's a great back-and-forth flow that carries one to gratitude.
The words that come from here reflect that connection and are spiritual by virtue of that connection. So perhaps, for you as well, where
you reside is within a way of being, such as gratitude, rather than a
specific corner of the body that symbolizes home.

A writing professor talks about his inner home using the ancient
Greek transliteration, *temenos*. Originally, the term referred to a secure
space surrounding a temple that was protected from intrusion from
the secular, political world. It was a place where a pilgrim could be free
from the concerns of that world and experience sanctuary in order to
reflect. When I hear the word *temenos* it makes me think of the Spanish word, *tenemos*, which means "we have." That's what we need from
home, to have it, to be in it. This professor writes, "I live in all the
places I have dreamed and dreamed of. A house of infinite windows
with a sparrow flying through in the blink of an eye." Perhaps the
place where you live most deeply is in an image from your life or from
a dream. Or it may be a location from your earliest childhood that
gives you a sense of home when you remember it.

Janis, a young people's librarian in California, said she almost
missed her bus stop pondering the question about where she lives. "I
go to my Polish grandmother's garden. The physical garden is gone.
There's a house where the garden used to be. But I can still go there.
It is surrounded by a long picket fence that my grandfather built. . . .
Everywhere there is a discovery. You can sit there and watch the garden and think. The gladiolas and delphiniums and dahlias and grasses
are so tall that you can forget that there's anyone else nearby. . . ."
When you settle into that place, you feel at peace, like you do after a
long day when you walk through your front door.

FOUNDATIONS OF HOME

Is there a cement slab holding your home in place, or are there piers dug far into the sand, on which your house sits with the tide rising and ebbing below? Consider what makes your inner dwelling place, from which you draw your words, safe and secure. Rose Lobel, a student in one of my workshops, wrote a poem using the metaphor of her childhood home.

We'll build a fire escape,
my father said,
of wood
attached to this brick building.
The ladder will slide down
over the incinerator.
We'll call it home.

After reading it, she told the group, with a kind of glee, "It's true!" Her father had built a wooden fire escape against the building's exterior brick wall. Luckily they never needed to flee a burning house on a wooden ladder.

The foundations of your childhood home may have been established by others—parents, teachers, even religious leaders. And those foundations contribute to the home you now have. But don't stop there, with an old definition of a place that's always new. Remake the foundations of your inner place so that it supports you as you need to be supported. What you create will likely include aspects of that childhood sense of inner self but not only that. It will also represent all you have become.

A lovely thing about childhood sensibility is how fluid it can be. The child will take in and accept what the adult might toss out. And the child is incredibly resilient, so even if your father built your family a wooden fire escape, your child's mind may have gilded it in gold and climbed to safety each time she needed to.

LOSING THE PLACE AND RETURNING

After learning that she had cancer—not for the first, but for the second time—my friend Wendy told me, "I felt as though the chair I'd been sitting on had lost its back. There was no support behind me and I had lost control. It was as if I didn't live anywhere." We may, in fact, have little control over many significant things in life, no matter how hard we try to put events and people in place and keep them from moving or changing. So much is beyond our jurisdiction. What we can control, to some degree, is how we respond to the changes that occur in our lives. And through spiritual writing you can stay in touch with the qualities of your inner home and experience fully how it feels to be there. Writing can support you through the times when you lose the back to your chair and all obvious signs of control. The writing keeps you aware.

When difficult things happen, like cancer or the loss of someone we love, it's pretty hard to feel our feet on the ground. We may feel like we're spiraling downward into emptiness. That's how my friend with cancer felt. I know I've felt that way, not because of cancer but for other reasons, many times. At those moments, before we can identify where we live, we may need to say that we feel as if we don't live anywhere, and write from that "nonplace."

My friend Carrie, who hasn't written for years, is grieving. Her husband of nearly twenty years up and left. He was there and then he wasn't. Just like that. Or so it seems. She called me to say, "I don't know where I am, but I do know I'm writing poems about being there. I hate this place. I really do. But my anger's being sucked up into this poetry. The work may in the end not be something I want to keep, but I don't care. Right now it's keeping me whole—somewhat, anyway."

Writing brings me back home. It may not occur the moment I sit down. I may need to write and put the notebook down and return to it several times before a sense of congruency with my inner self takes place. But through the practice of truth telling, it does return, and I begin to feel a settling down as my words take hold on the paper and stitch me back into place.

THE IMPORTANCE OF LISTENING

For writing to be a spiritual practice, you must make manifest the life of the soul, give voice to the place where you live. When I am in sync with it, my writing comes from that place, where I am most truly alive. To write from within, you have to listen for what's there. And listen deeply. It's more than your ears doing this listening. This attention requires all of your senses, your complete awareness. Then the outside enters in. Through listening, I can define and clarify my vision. There's no rigidity unless I block myself. When I remain open, the inner world directs me to write.

If I "listen" to rain on only the most external level of self, I might just notice that it's wet and cold and write my poem from there, bringing in only the concrete details of the physical world. That kind of writing remains on the surface and doesn't hold my attention, not as a writer or a reader. But as I bring the weather in on more internal levels, I notice more about it and my reactions to it. The more I enter the well within, the more I experience and am affected by the outside world as it is truly part of my inner one. I might feel the dampness of rain at soul level. The listening pose I enter when I hear the rain might cause me to listen more deeply and to remember the rain and how I've known it before.

When we write from within, listening wholly, we may be given what seem like contradictions to follow. But there is a great integrity that one finds by meandering down the path. Bowlfuls of words are there. Enough to fill a tree's hollow, a hungry mouth, a well. When the well seems to have run dry, it probably just needs to be fed by the spring of creativity—a spring that's yours and God's. To write is to follow a calling to feed the well. We'll talk more about this well and nurturing it as we go. This book exists so that you may contact and more deeply live within that place, respect its wisdom, and find the language that issues from there. And through writing, you may bring together the many aspects of your life, finding the spiritual essence that links them. We'll discover how writing brings us closer to the inner home, how it helps us know the spiritual truths that are there.

My friend Marion spends more time by herself than anyone I know. She lives alone (with a few felines), works away from home only three days a week, lives modestly. Sometimes she tells me she's "going on retreat." When I was first getting to know her and she said this, I imagined her packing a few essentials—toothbrush, comb and sweater, a journal and colored pencils—and kissing her cats good-bye and driving up a muddy dirt road through the trees to an austere retreat house with walls that let the wind in. Not the case. What she means is she won't answer the phone or have visitors. On those days she's going to be more alone than at other times. I've learned this from her. On days when I need most to be on the first floor of my building, I just don't answer the phone and I keep the blinds that face the street side of the house shut. If someone knocks at the door, I get very quiet and ignore the sound. It's a bit difficult to do this because I live with someone and we like to be together. So I save my retreat days for when my sweetheart's at work or backpacking in the Sierra and I've got a day I can take off from teaching. To nurture the whole of my soul, I need to pull in and tend to my inner garden.

Last week I took a retreat and drove four hours along freeways at seventy-five mph and onto a winding road that goes through the tiny towns of Esparto, Rumsey, and Guinda. Down a rutted dirt road, over a wood-slat bridge, through a gate for "Registered Guests Only," past a road sign that reads "Time to Slow Down," and up to an old house where I parked my car, checked in, and didn't speak to anyone for sixty hours. I walked in the country, up dirt paths and past fallen barns. I sat down on a hillside in the sun and felt spring enter my body one cell at a time. I leaned back on the hill and looked up to the sky, reciting bits and pieces of poems—a line from Osip Mandelstam ("Take from my palms, for your delight and joy, a little honey . . .") and Anna Akhmatova ("I don't speak with anyone for a week . . ."). The poems got me to settle farther into my "home" each moment. It's often through reading poems that I return to myself. And back in my room

I wrote with the floodgates open wide. I didn't *try* to do anything except not work, and that wasn't too hard as I'd left all sign of "work" at home in my study. In fact "try" and "do" didn't come up in the same thought the whole time. It's not always that way. Sometimes it's a struggle to just be with myself and listen, but not on this journey.

After those days alone, I felt somewhat more able to move in the world with more to give. Really, I could have used about a week there but that will have to wait for another time, one with more relaxation time and more money. I'm grateful for the days I did have and the writing that came. I've been carrying the quiet I had in those hills with me everywhere since then. Each day I spend a few moments consciously remembering it, feeling the home within me as it felt in those quiet hours, and I linger there.

THE LANDSCAPE OF THE SELF
Art and Necessity

The playwright Lanford Wilson once said, "Art is born out of, among other things, necessity. Writing a play for me is like walking down this landscape of the self." Reading that, I see a man with a walking stick and a knapsack on his back, striding alongside his bones, noticing the details of his inner landscape—blood flowing through his river-veins, the pulsations of muscles, ideas, and feelings. Necessity and self and the body all go together. We easily recognize the necessities of the body; we can't get by long without doing so.

But what about the necessities of the inner self? Our art may or may not pay the bills or bring fame, but its necessity is clear to those of us who practice it. For some, the imperative to make art, to take the walk into the canyons and mesas of the self and out again, is as basic as breathing, eating, and sleeping. If I don't write, I don't feel well; I'm out of my own groove. This need is not a selfish one any more than the need for air, water, food, or shelter is. This is a requirement for being the whole self.

I think we've got it a bit backward these days, having convinced ourselves that our physical needs include the possession of more and more things, like a little child who says to his mom when they're at the grocery store in the candy section, "I need this," pointing to all that's sugary. Herman Hesse said, "I wanted to live in accord with the promptings of my true self. Why is that so very difficult?" We've revisualized the need for the whole self and its promptings, the connection with soul and God, as a need for inanimate objects, the newest computer gadget, as if having it would really take away our inner gnawing for meaning. There's a blue sweater I saw last weekend when my teenage goddaughter Kyle and I went shopping for her birthday. I can't afford it. I want it, having tried it on and liking how it looked and felt against my skin. I would enjoy wearing it, no doubt. But that good feeling is nothing next to the sense of the divine I experience in prayer or when writing. The invisible ultimately warms me more than a blue silk sweater.

Looking at the prosperity of much of the United States these days, I sometimes wonder what it would be like to feel called to do something that brought me big money. Living on dwindling book advances and a little bit of teaching can be unnerving, but for who I am, it would be swindling myself to give up poetry in exchange for real estate or banking. I'm fortunate to take my inner home with me wherever I go and earn a living from it. What I'm doing is my true work, difficult as it may be at times. I've always been determined to do work that keeps me in line with my inner self and where I feel I may be of service to others. Teaching and writing have always been my way in the world.

When we are who we feel called to be, the foundation of the self is greater, more substantial and solid; we're not closed off. Many writers, painters, musicians, and dancers recognize art's role in their lives as the activity that connects them physically, spiritually, emotionally, intellectually, politically, and socially. Making art and being in this home of the self is a way for the many parts of the self to be in conversation with each other. It facilitates the life of our spiritual selves.

The scholar Ellen Dissanayake believes that art serves a biological necessity, that it's a behavior and, as such, is not the "exclusive possession of just a select few; rather, like swimming or lovemaking, art is a behavior potentially available to everyone." If we consider art something we do, a process we can engage in, then we don't have to wait for a stamp of someone else's approval to do it. We just have to be called to it and respond to that inclination. It improves my physical, emotional, and spiritual health. It makes me a nicer person. To be able to be in dialogue with the various aspects of the self is one way in which being and doing art can help us to survive. Merleau-Ponty said, "Your act is you." It could also be said that your art is you.

When you ignore this need, even if it's only at the level of what you'd consider desire, the inner self may remain hidden and go underground. If making art can help you to feel congruent and connected, not making it may cause you to feel off balance. If creature comforts and personal wealth are representative of success, what about the soul? Financial success is a narrow view of what it can mean to lead a successful life. What's the definition of soul success for you? Can it be measured on the outside, via tangible results? Or could the inner workings of the self, living within oneself deeply, and the non-materialistic manifestations of such a life be determinants of true success?

The poet Robinson Jeffers lived in Carmel, California, long before it was a tourist spot designed to attract the affluent. His land went right up to the Pacific. His home, which he named Tor House, is still there, maintained by a foundation that offers tours of the property. During his lifetime he became well known for his poetry. When I walk by his home, I like to look up at the tower that he built for his wife and think about the fame he got for laying down the stones and building the tower. On a tour led by his granddaughter, we were taken up into the tower. At some spots along the narrow staircase you can fit through only by turning sideways. At the top there's a room with a desk. I imagine Una Jeffers at that desk, writing beside the window. The tower didn't make Jeffers money or bring him success in the larger world. It was made for love.

Our culture suffers from a negation of the inner self, the god-self. We don't often witness that self in each other. It's important to know who we are, who others are, where our tender spots are. These are not mechanized needs, nor needs that can be met in front of computer screens. When a primary need is ignored, it may express itself in destructive ways. Our preoccupation with material possessions is unsettling. The violence on the part of young people must be, in part, a call for attention to the soul. There are children I know who, after school, instead of playing on the street or at the homes of friends, park themselves in front of the computer and play games. Carl Jung said, "The cat neglected becomes the unconscious tiger." We're seeing a number of neglected cats these days. When the need to attend to the inner self isn't modeled as valuable, when art and the spiritual life aren't integrated into the culture, the self may choose destructive routes for attention, such as reckless displays of violence.

It's not that soul writing by itself is going to solve cultural problems. But it can support the inner being and widen the ground we stand on, giving us more foundation. Through writing we can walk the landscape and maintain connections between self, God, and the spiritual nature of life and find a wholeness where it once was lacking.

TRANSFORMATION OF THE SELF

May Sarton, a writer who lived alone for many years in Maine in a house by the sea, wrote, "The fact that a middle-aged woman, without any vestige of family left, lives in this house in a silent village and is responsible to only her own soul means something. The fact that she is a writer and can tell where she is and what it is like on the pilgrimage inward can be of some comfort." Turning to her journals, the first of which, *Journal of a Solitude*, I found shortly after high school, was like coming across a path that led to the way in. Her way in, yes, but the journals demonstrated to me—as did other literature, like the poems of Rainer Maria Rilke—that other people resided in this inward place and were compelled to name it and through writing to illuminate it, question it, be transformed by it. Reading them gave validity to a search for like-minded seekers I'd begun as a young child. I always felt that several worlds existed simultaneously and that I was a part, even in miniscule ways, of them all. Not so simple as inner world–outer world, but world within world, inner within outer and vice versa, and nature world, people world, inanimate object world, the world of moving things and of the stationary.

When I was a child my father occasionally spoke to me about light, particularly how the color of the buildings in certain neighborhoods in lower Manhattan were affected by late afternoon light. We'd be walking together, and he'd stop me with a hand on my shoulder and say, "Look," as he stared down the street. There was no parade going by, no movie star getting out of a limo; it was the light he was referring to, how it changed what he saw and gave everything a glow and warmed the colors. He had a tone of voice that was reserved for those observations alone. I wouldn't otherwise have noticed that last bit of musty brightness before the dark comes. I must have been no more than four years old the first time my father pointed out the light. He wore suit pants, a well-pressed shirt, and a fine narrow-brimmed hat. He looked elegant. He was drawing me to notice more than the actual light, to find a quality of attention that came from deep inside, that was about a sorrow of sorts. The ending of day reminded him of other endings, I think, and how fleeting intense moments were, the importance of recognizing the beauty in something before it fled. I knew it was about the outside coming in, and I felt he was opening a door for me into a place where we both lived. And that he was bringing an intimate part of himself forward, pulling me in close to him. What I heard was: this matters—pay attention to the details of the world and yourself.

Sarton, my father, and others got me thinking about transformation and the meaning of living in this inner place. I witnessed my father change in those moments: his voice slowed down, and he became calm; his passionate nature was more focused than usual. He was less agitated than he often was, kinder, and in that kindness he made more room for me beside him. "How hungry the world still is for clues about those stepping stones, the final destination of a self transformed by creative life. How is it accomplished? What is the imagination's link to life?" wrote May Sarton. How is a self transformed through regular dialogue with the inner home? It is not only the creative act itself that is influenced by deep attention, it is the whole of life. My father had once been a painter, but for many reasons I don't know he didn't continue to paint. Still, he dwells in that creative space of the inner life. He sees people from that place and they are drawn to him, to being seen.

When we recognize the inner self in both ourselves and others, our compassion grows because we see a well-rounded picture that includes the girth and depth of a life. We see with our still, small hearts that open naturally to others. Intuitiveness grows, sensory awareness increases. An awareness of God is not only found when entering church doors; when we attend to the inner dwelling place, we notice God everywhere. The inner connectedness between matter and nonmatter, between time and space, past and future, are clear.

WRITING FROM HOME

To make a prairie it takes a clover and one bee,
One clover, and a bee,
And revery.
The revery alone will do,
If bees are few.

EMILY DICKINSON, from *The Collected Poems of Emily Dickinson*

You don't have to have everything. There's a difference between everything and enough. You may stay away from writing when you think you don't have everything or when you think what you have isn't enough. Maybe you can't bring revery just yet. Maybe you can bring one bee or a piece of clover. Whatever it is, whatever you have within yourself, consider it enough, and that the Spirit behind, above, and below you will do the rest. Your house is enough; it's got plenty of floor space, great windows. The goods stored in your cupboards are all you need. The place you live will give you what's necessary for your writing life. Notice how different it feels in your body to have enough. Try it. Say to yourself, "It's enough. What I have is what I need."

You don't even have to wholly believe in yourself as a writer or as a soulful, spiritual being. Bring your doubts; they too will fuel the work and get your hands into the mud and muck. You just need one quality: desire, inclination—a stone in your shoe that you can't shake out though you've sat down on the ground, untied the lace, turned your shoe upside down, and shaken it vigorously. There's a knocking at the door of yourself and even when you walk into another room you can still hear the rat-a-tat.

You know what life you live, where you've been, and what you see, hear, smell, taste, and touch. You know what you love. That's your essence. There are words behind the living and the loving even if you don't know the words. Trust the words that are most true for you as you go past the bends in the road of what's not true, or almost true, or kind of true; past what your mother thought should be true for you, or what your teacher told you over and over about tact, or what your uncle said about the necessity of throwing the first punch. Go beyond the others and into yourself.

Think about belonging for a moment. Think about the things that belong to you and to what you belong. As a girl, I felt I didn't belong. I belonged to my family, yes, only sometimes, but to no one and nowhere beyond that. Many of us feel that sense of strangeness in relation to others at times. That sense of not belonging, or not being a part, was one of the first awarenesses I had of belonging: to belong to not belonging. And out of that I built my definitions and discovered where my connections would be found.

Start anywhere. What rhythm do you belong to? What region is yours? What footfalls take you into the days? What sleep carries you through the night? Is the territory of your mind icy and well cornered, or is it limpid and shadowed? Do you belong to another? Is she long-limbed? Is he the grandfather of a hidden quarry? Does your belonging to another make you more of who you are than you were before this person entered your life and mind?

It's not only people and places we belong to, but words, their sounds, and their meanings. There are words we've carried with us for years. You may remember the first sound that certain words made when you read them to yourself and then said them aloud. The word *curriculum* is a dry word in meaning; there's no taste to it. But when I first said it, as a kid having, I'm sure, heard my parents use it but not remembering that, I thought I'd made it up. I had no idea what it really meant. I experienced it only as sound. It's not a word I can love; it's too empty and cumbersome for that. But it's there from a summer when I was five playing in the New York heat with my favorite cousin. The word *Tiparillo* is another early one. It came from a sexy television commercial, and it was an early lesson about the connection between language and seduction, the tone of the cigarette saleswoman's voice, the slight swagger to her hips. I used to say that word over and over until I stumbled on it and could not, for the time, say it again. It wasn't till later that I felt myself belong to words like *foxglove* and *magenta*. The words *Marry me* always made me cringe until last summer. Now those words too reside in that inner place, which had to change in shape to contain them.

Hang out and linger long with the words that you belong to and that belong to you. There is nothing too small to attend to. A single syllable can hold your attention if you give in to it. The compact phrases that you speak to yourself daily, the individual words you roll around on your tongue. See where they take you: *hinge, key, trailer, ragged, running down the road alone, calling home, river's edge, grace. . . .*

When you see the sun set, it has already dropped below the horizon more than eight minutes before you see it fall. The light we see at night from the nearest stars takes four and a half years to get here, and from the most distant stars in the farthest galaxies, it can take billions of years. Think of having that to draw from when you write, your own distant light that ignited years ago and has been traveling through the path of your life to get here right now. How the past comes forward into the future and how you see it as now. You might take that light and the particles of history in it, and follow that to the page. Bring it all into your inner home so you can write it as you desire.

When we write from our deepest selves, having entered that sequestered inner sanctum, we find what's most true for who we are. The novelist Anne Rice says, "Writers write about what obsesses them. You draw those cards. I lost my mother when I was fourteen. My daughter died at the age of six. I lost my faith as a Catholic. When I'm writing, the darkness is always there. I go where the pain is." We encounter our obsessions, our dragons, our Achilles' heel (or, in this case, perhaps it should be called our Achilles' *heal*). Because, in fact, what we come to is what needs attention in one way or another. What we find there is what we need to heal. And those are the treasures we bring to our art.

Sometimes, I think I want a different story. I want a new origin. I grow tired of my own story, my own obsessions and pain, my own greed for telling a particular thing in a particular kind of way. I think I want to live elsewhere, in another interior space. But to turn from my own inner spiritual truth would not bring me to good writing; it would distance me from that possibility as well as cut me off from who I am. And cut off from ourselves, we have no foundation whatsoever—nowhere to stand, nowhere to move forward from.

Some days, when I encounter only the darkness when I am praying for light, I know what I must do, for authenticity is to be with what's there, whether I like it or not, whether it's politically correct or correct in terms of what my family would like me to say or not to say. While working on an anthology of poetry, I contacted a newly published writer to ask if I could reprint a poem of hers in my collection. First she shrieked excitedly into the phone, and the next words out of her mouth were, "But, what will my mother think?" Then quickly she said, "Oh, well," and gave me permission to use her poem. Our finest work comes when we speak from the residence of the soul. And often it's the work that rests (if it rests at all) on the edge, because that's where we as readers also want to be met. Like Lanford Wilson, we walk along the "landscape of the self."

The wound that I write out of is, at times, the "don't leave me" wound. Even though I haven't been left in a very long time, it's still the place that hurts. It's not really about being left by *someone* but a fear of being left by God, of being left without that inner sanctuary and descending into the long black cave where I have fallen before.

HEART LINES

One's spiritual self is also the most deeply social self and political self, because everything we are ultimately initiates from the soul and thus connects us to others. When our awareness is lit in this deepest of places, we can ultimately make little distinction between the individual self and the collective; at the core we're one and the same. The sacred interconnectedness between beings is paramount. The soul knows that whatever may make you unique, your essential, authentic self is also made up of what makes you the same as all others.

In an interview in the *Paris Review*, the Israeli poet Yehuda Amichai said:

Real poets, I think, turn the outer world into the inner world and vice versa. Poets always have to be outside, in the world—a poet can't close himself in his studio. His workshop is in his head, and he has to be sensitive to words and how words apply to realities. It's a state of mind. A poet's state of mind is seeing the world with a kind of double exposure, seeing undertones and overtones, seeing the world as it is. Every intelligent person, whether he's an artist or not—a mathematician, a doctor, a scientist—possesses a poetic way of seeing and describing the world.

Through writing from the home within you'll discover your own poetic ways of seeing. Even when writers are at their desks, if they're writing from their deep selves, the outside comes in. One would have to live in an awfully deep cave to remain stoical and unaffected. Only those with closed hearts can remain immune to the events of the outer world. If we're making art, we can't remain completely isolated. Art opens our hearts not only to our own experiences but to those of all others. The soul is porous. It has no boundaries. Writing spiritually draws from us our holistic ways of knowing of the worlds within and without. We write from our range of experience, bringing the outer world in and the inner world out.

For the Notebook 1

WHERE DO YOU LIVE?

To locate the place where you live inside yourself, free yourself from distractions. You might sit very still, or, if movement is your element, go for a silent walk, without human company. Quiet will help you find the bowl-like hollowness of the place within where you are most at home. Soften your vision. Your outward glance isn't pointed nor is your inward one. This takes a little time being by yourself. If you're sitting in a room, give yourself a half hour or so on the couch or the floor without bright lights or the telephone but with a blank book open on your lap and a good pen nearby. Your children will have to fend for themselves. The curtains may stay open later than usual. Focus on your most true self, and just notice what is there. Something is. Listen for the sound of arrival that tells you when you're home. A constant hum like the ocean at a distance may greet you or a small voice that beckons. You might take a journey through interior vaults. You might feel a guttural sound coming from the back of your throat. This is the where of your inner self, your home, the place you listen and love from.

Where do you feel a sense of home within yourself? How tall or deep or wide a place is it? Just be there, without judgment. As I mentioned earlier in this chapter, my home place is just below my heart, above my belly. And you, as well, may have a clear sense of an actual, physical location of the home within. Is it your head? Your heart? Your arms when they swing? The palms of your hands? Or perhaps your sense of home is located more in the quietness of being than in an area of your body. What's the temperature there? How deep or shallow, near or far is this home? What takes you there? What pulls you away? Does sound connect you to your home within or does a color? Begin by writing what this inner domicile is like. Accept whatever words arrive that describe it or that don't describe it: you may find writing what your home within isn't to be a way of clarifying what it is. You can easily do this exercise in a half hour; you may not get all the details but you'll gain a greater awareness. You may cover only a small amount of paper with words—a page isn't too short—or you may find that to write your way into this place you need a few pieces of paper. Write from the inside out; rather than determining in advance how much you'll write, begin to let the writing write you, deciding when to stop by how the process feels. This is how we'll continue from here. I could tell you to write five pages, but you might need ten; or a simple paragraph will do. Some days a half hour will give me a few words, but at other times I'm surprised by how much I can say in a short while.

You may wish to return to this exercise often as you further your relationship with the inner home. Metaphorically hang pictures, put dishes in the cabinet, pull the broom out from the closet. Then begin the journey of writing the words that come from this place, the words that are most truly yours. You're on your way.

For the Notebook 2

GETTING BACK HOME

When you feel at a distance from your soul-self, how do you get back? You might begin to notice what draws you to your self after feeling pulled away by the complexities of leading an early-twenty-first-century life. When do you feel nearest not only to yourself, but to the inner self in the people you're closest to? And what's the difference between being near and being far? Take out your notebook and begin paying attention to what draws you home and what it's like to be away. This one's a quickie; try writing for ten minutes. Then, get up, stretch, and know you've written something you can return to should you wish.

CHAPTER 2

THE INNER CONSTELLATION
Ways of Knowing

And now Tangle felt there was something in her knowledge
which was not in her understanding.
George MacDonald

I've known all my life that I could take a bunch of words
and throw them up in the air and they would
come down just right.
Truman Capote

A poem should almost successfully escape the intellect.
Wallace Stevens

What do you know? And how do you know it? How many ways do you have for knowing? And what does it mean to know? Do you trust the veracity and wisdom of your knowledge? What do you know of God and the life of the soul? What belief do you put in what you know? How did that belief become yours? When do you acknowledge and accept your knowing? Do you love the complexity of your awareness? How do you know yourself as a writer? And what ways of knowing do you rely on when you write?

GROWING ONIONS

Outside his home in a yard the size of a postage stamp, my father has a garden. Although he is seventy-seven, it's his first garden, and he's got all his favorite vegetables growing—garlic, peppers, onions, oregano, nearly everything one needs for a good Italian meal, except the pasta. My father gardens like he knows what he's doing, but I have to wonder otherwise. How could he do something for the first time late in life and actually know how to do it without books or instruction? As a boy in Queens, in the yard in front of his house in Astoria, a block from the East River, did he spend enough time watching his father till the ground and tend carefully to the vegetables and flowers that he learned to garden then and has retained it, kept it secreted away in his mind? Does memory work this way? Or is there more than memory at work? Do we know through love?

It's August in my garden, where onions grow amid kale, basil, zucchini, and lettuce. Everything is truly becoming itself; the lettuce heads are enormous; the kale is as tall as I am. The zucchini pushes everything out of its way. The onions have been in the ground since early June. Are they ready for the sauté pan yet? I ask my dad. "Not yet," he says. "The tops need to be dry and brown. It would help, too, if you were to mound some good dirt on them as they begin to push at the ground. Keep 'em in the ground a little longer; that way they'll get really big."

That's pretty sophisticated for a novice gardener, and not an instruction I find in the *Sunset Western Garden Book*. So I ask, "Pop, how do you know that?" He gets a sheepish look. He's a little embarrassed, and surprised, I think, to have been asked. I love to see that expression—it's like I've caught him right when and where he wanted to be caught. "Nineteen forty-six. I was on the train, coming home from the army, out of Amarillo, Texas. For miles I did nothing but look out the window, and that's what the farmers did then, there along the route of the train. They bent down and mounded dirt around the onions growing in their fields."

A young man travels home from the army after the end of World War II on a train crossing state line after state line. Here's a man who wants to get back to the house on Nineteenth Street at the corner of Twenty-First Avenue—to his mother, father, and sister, and beyond the gate, to his friend with a pet raccoon and all the guys who'll congregate again down at the filling station. And a girlfriend I know nearly nothing about, though I did hear he gave her a ring. A man who wants to get back to his future that will have him studying art and psychology, not horticulture; a future that will make him a young family, take him from New York City to Chicago, and on to California. Years later, he's retired and lives in a condominium with a yard that gets lots of summer sun. An old man now, he holds memory and, among all of it, unforgotten knowledge of what can happen under the soil, where transformation is mostly kept from view. As he'd seen long ago from a train window, he mounds some good dirt over the bulb of the hidden onion, firm and pushing up, large under his palm.

My father's memories are not mine but they have infused me for more than forty years. They are a part of my fiber. Even the memories I don't actually know, the stories I'll never hear. The same is true for everyone: what we are conscious of and what we aren't aware we know both exist in real ways, ways that influence and affect our thoughts, feelings, behavior, and the art we make.

A few weeks after the onion conversation, a small package arrives in the mail, flat along the edges with an oval-shaped lump in the middle. Unwrapping the gift, the smell hits me first: onion, of course. My father has sent me one of his first. Wrapped in plastic, it has a large tag attached with bold, red letters: "Uno, Prized Red Torpedo Onion." Off to the side: "For your dining pleasure." It's thick skinned and purple. Dirt from the garden falls from the packing. For dinner I sauté it with mushrooms, garlic, and a little red wine. Eating supper in the near dark, I'm quiet, imagining my father looking for miles through train windows.

Growing in my dad's yard are not just onions, but the time he spent in the army, the train ride home, the farmers' fields, his father's onions. My mother's voice, that's out there too, and a host of other things I know nothing about. So, my father is growing the past's soul and spirit in that little garden patch, and the memories are our bond. They link us back through time to who he once was and who my grandparents were and all we might have become, if this life had been different. If *his* life had been different . . . I start the sentence but can't quite finish it. Maybe that's why that onion tasted so good last night. It was tinged by more than garlic, more than the evening's light.

WAYS OF KNOWING

A psychic once told my friend Jim that it seemed he didn't value his intelligence because of the package that he perceived it came in—a huge, beat-up refrigerator box. Your storehouse may not be fancy, but it serves you and it gets you where you need to be. There's more in your wealth of knowledge, be it a refrigerator box or coin purse, than you may have realized. Your knowledge is made up of a constellation of many ways of perceiving. Through writing we can deepen our awareness and learn to rely on ways of knowing that maybe we hadn't before considered informative, worthy, or reliable. If, as health author Anne Kent Rush said, "Creativity is really the structuring of magic," then what we're structuring are our perceptions, our knowledge, our experiences, and our souls. God enters into that mix. The magic is in this blending and the surprising way in which the words come together to make something new. Hard work goes into the making, but there needs to be room, as well, for the inspired and the unpredictable.

I'm leafing through the magazine section of a recent Sunday *New York Times*. On page forty, I'm stopped by the word *YOU* in large block letters in the middle of the page. "Are they talking to me?" I wonder. The piece is titled, "What We Use to Learn About Ourselves." The word *you* is a bull's-eye surrounded by concentric circles divided into little squares, more than 150 of them, and inside each one is an image and a word or two: "Jokes," "Late Lunches," "Celibacy," "The F Train." I'll bet you could think of an additional 150 ways that you use to know yourself and the world. Through all the details, the large and small events of our lives, we gain knowledge. Often, even the instantaneous moments that flash by teach us something and add to the wealth we draw from when writing.

In this chapter, we'll look at some of our many ways of knowing and see how an integration of them can further our writing practice and help us welcome the spiritual into it. That my father could begin gardening as an old man without books on the subject tells me he opened himself to more than just his intellect. To believe in our knowing requires faith. For me, this is a faith that's less about believing in myself and more about faith in the inner workings of the soul. Not only is belief a suspension of doubt, it's a suspension of rational knowing; it's a belief in something larger than the individual. We can welcome the unknown if we take a leap of faith into what we think we don't know or couldn't know. Then we get to our greatest knowing. It's when I feel afraid of this leap that my writing lags and becomes as dull as the silver bowl I leave unpolished until I remember what it can be.

Writer Susan Griffin speaks of what many of us go through when she says, "I am certain before I begin writing a piece that I will not be able to put sentences together, or worse, that all I have to say has been said before, that there is no purpose, that there is no intrinsic authority to my own words." That's the initial distrust of knowing. When my ego, or the internal critic, whom we'll discuss later, runs the show and I try to control my writing in an orderly, linear manner, I get stopped up, much like a clogged sink. Faith is my plumber. When I forget my soul, the writing loses heart.

It's not only our individual doubt about our knowing, inner selves that can block writing; there's also a culture of distrust and hesitation that can affect us. Writer Jan Clausen reminds us that we've got to be our own advocates for our work. "I actually believe that most of life is probably an obstacle to writing for any writer. The world just does not need your gratuitous product. You must never quit insisting." *Never quit insisting.* We can bring our ways of knowing and the need to write to support our work and counter what we may feel the world hands us. If you need to write, could that be enough? Could you trust that as a way of knowing what's true?

Our various ways of knowing include spiritual knowledge, body knowledge, school and book learning, and life experiences. We know through whom and what we love that loving teaches us. There's the knowing we get from what is said, but sometimes the knowing we arrive at from what is not said is greater. The images and stories of dreams present their awarenesses to us. We can verify our knowledge of certain things in the past. But there are also the things we can't set a date and time to, that we *feel* have happened, that we *know* somewhere within a mix of mind and body, heart and soul. That knowing counts as well. Might it be just as real? The future is what hasn't happened, yet aren't there times you *know* bits and pieces of that as well? The spiritual self knows what the intellectual self cannot because the intellectual self wants verifiable proof that can be substantiated logically. The intellect wants something to hold in its hand, but the spiritual self knows in a more subliminal, quiet, less compact way. But because something cannot be held in your hand, is it less real or more?

The rational mind will reason its way through a situation. It knows how to think and stores the information we need: facts and figures, names and places. It's always moving toward resolution. If we rely solely on intellect and deductive thinking, we limit our potential. Our energy can get stuck there, and we may close ourselves off to other ways of knowing. The Buddhist writer and teacher Toni Packer notes that, "When energy knots up high in the head, entangled in thoughts and images and proclamations imagined to be real, the whole body becomes immobilized with emotionality. It cannot perceive that it is an integral part of everything else that's going on around it. It feels encapsulated, enclosed, isolated." When I get stuck on one idea or focused on knowing only through logical thought, I have the sensation that my head is inflated like a balloon that's bobbing along, separate from the rest of me. Every other switch leading me to consciousness is turned off, and no juice can get through. No longer do I feel a sense of fluidity and connection. I'm not open to change but have become frozen and steadfast. The breath is often what brings me back to my body and my range of possible ways of knowing. I have to get back to the self, to the physical, to feel connected. When I breathe with an awareness to that, I know I have a body and that one feeling isn't my entire identity. I know that God resides in the flux and rhythm.

Body Knowing

If you attend to the awareness of your body, you'll get different knowledge than what logical thought can give you. Your body knows when it's full or tired. The body and the emotional self relate, are often in dialogue. Try recording that conversation sometime. Emotions can bring the body and mind together. When happy, you may skip or jump; there's that smile crossing your face. You may have to get up and move, take a little walk, attend to your awareness at a slow pace to read what the body says and attune yourself to how body and emotion interact.

What does your body know? Its ways of knowing will not desert you. Its knowing remains true and will be enhanced through your attention and reliance. The musician Jerry Garcia once said, "In the water you're weightless. It's so silent you're like a thought. When I begin to relax, the songs start happening in my head." The body needs to relax to float. If you're stiff and afraid, the water will not hold you well and you'll flail and splash. Little thought or fresh writing comes out of that. But if you have faith in the floating, faith in the water, alliances are made from that. The mind needs its floating. The artist Ann Hamilton represented the United States at the Venice Biennale in the summer of 1999. She created a large installation she titled *myein*, which is Greek for the contracting of the pupil of the eye and also the root word of *mystery*. Her piece surrounded the U.S. pavilion with panes of textured glass that made a rippling effect like water. Inside the building, a rose-colored powder sifted down the walls. In a *New York Times* article, Hamilton described the creative experience similarly to Garcia as being something of the body, not distinct from it. "You float yourself in an atmosphere that makes you think. It's not that you get ideas directly." Floating is a physical experience; we know it in the body. It happens when we're open to our many ways of knowing and receive what they have to give us.

A few months before the exhibit in Venice was due to open, Hamilton still didn't know exactly what she would make. "Everyone's asking me, 'Do you know what you're doing?' And they're surprised when I say no. But I've never known at this stage. In some ways, I feel I must know somewhere in my body. Part of the process is trusting that." When we trust our body awareness, we can relax into the unknown of the creative process and float in it, let the body and the mind float in it. Creativity is about being in the process. The process comes before the product, and to rush to product stifles process and thus the end result. Recently, a friend who's an interior designer asked me, "How many hours till your book's finished?" "Hours," I bolted back at her, "Hours? You want to know how many more hours it will take to complete? I have absolutely no idea." When I began working on the book, I'd tell myself, "OK, write for four hours a day." And I would. Soon four hours became five, but on days when the writing was like walking through drying cement three would about do me in. Now, for the past few months, I write not in time but in process. The writing's what determines when to stop, not the clock. It's like the writing now has its own identity and time, and that's what I follow. It's a knowing that comes from inside the act, not from outside.

I know it in my body as well as in my heart and mind. Poet and novelist Kate Braverman knows it this way, "If you are writing anything that matters, your body tells you where to stop. Writing a poem is physical." In Chapter 9 we'll talk more about not knowing and the power that resides in that.

Perceptions

Through our senses we discover the outer world and receive information. When I touch my lover's face and feel the bristles on his cheeks, I feel an emotional and physical response. The bursting beads of a pomegranate open my eyes wider as the tangy-sweet taste hits my tongue. What we know of the world is based on our perceptions of it. And those perceptions are the result of who we are and everything that we've known before this moment. The scientist Richard Gregory notes, "We not only believe what we see, to some extent we see what we believe." How you perceive the color green may not be how your best friend does. The sound of the mockingbird may soothe you and drive your brother crazy. Poets strive to illuminate their ways of knowing the world so that readers may enter the fleshed-out nuances and particularities anew. K. C. Cole, in her book *First You Build a Cloud,* writes, "Perception, after all, is a very *active* process. We do not just sit around waiting for information to rain down on us. We go out and get it. In the process we alter it and even create it." We also go within and get it. Our senses may contradict each other; our eyes say it's a sunny day but the wind against our legs says, "Put a sweater on!" So we sort the information out and dress accordingly.

The Knowing Heart

Our emotions give us ways of knowing. In his poem "The Waking," Theodore Roethke says, "We think by feeling. What is there to know?" Emotions register experience through how we were affected in the past. How we know through sorrow may be different than how we know through compassion. What our anger tells us may contradict what our joy insists on saying. A particular emotion is like a watercolor wash and we see the world through that color. Some degrees of various emotions are so strong the world may temporarily become opaque. We tap into our deepest knowing when we are attentive and attuned to the soul-self, and regard our emotional selves as part of that.

Intuitive Awareness

Your intuition may tell you what you couldn't know any other way. My friend Jasmin greeted me at the library, having come with her children to the community writing class I lead there once a month. When everyone had settled into writing, she and I stepped into the hall for a brief visit. I was trying to listen to her but I was also looking at the students writing—who was gliding along, who was stuck, who needed more paper, and so on. What I thought I heard Jasmin say was, "I miss carrying." She missed carrying what, I wondered and imagined a bushel of fruit, a baby in her arms. Then I looked at her face. Her eyes were tearing. She said, "I know it's not medically possible, but I knew the instant I was pregnant; I could feel the cells divide, and later I knew the moment her spirit was gone. I called the clinic to schedule an ultrasound. They asked, 'Are you bleeding?' 'No.' 'Are you cramping?' 'No, but I know I'm losing my baby.'" And sure enough, she was. We often know what's impossible to know. But what is inauthentic isn't knowing the "impossible," it's the idea that we can't know it. I read this section to another friend and her face got light pink as I read. She said, "Me, too. I knew as I began to miscarry. I was at the high school tutoring some students. Something was suddenly different inside me, though there weren't yet any outward signs." The problem is when we believe an outside authority over our own intuitive, spiritual knowing and give up soul knowing for "facts" because we think they are more true, that our innate knowing isn't enough to bank on. What if your innate knowing were verifiable but you had to use a system of verification other than external facts and what others told you? Then would you believe yourself?

Holy Knowing

In the seventies, the psychologist Edith Sullwold worked with a six-year-old boy who'd been adopted at birth and was displaying violent, troubling behavior. When the boy came into Sullwold's office for the first time, he introduced himself to her using, not his proper name, but calling himself Eagle Eye. During the course of their work together, Sullwold invited him to make up stories. During their first session, he worked at the sand tray and made an American Indian village and a cowboy town. He told his therapist, "I am an Indian." As their work together progressed, he continued to tell her stories that included Native American motifs. In response to one sand-tray scene, he said, "I was a brave baby Indian where I was born in the desert." The boy's healing began with the telling of imaginal stories.

His parents had no information about their son's heritage but Sullwold thought it was time to find out. His parents discovered that his birth mother was a Mexican Indian woman. This confirmed what Eagle Eye obviously already knew. He'd been dipping into his core knowledge and making connections he didn't have conscious knowledge of. Through working with his imagination and with an adult who had faith in that imagination, Eagle Eye made contact with his cultural heritage. His work with Sullwold ended when he was able to integrate this primal, interior knowing into his life with his adoptive parents. He didn't give up his knowing; he embraced it fully.

Imagination engages the deepest part of our being, and it is there the spiritual self resides. This is a kind of holy knowing. The well of this knowing draws from the earth, from the shared knowing of all people, from personal experience—both what we're conscious of and what we're not. The richness of this well never runs dry. Even when our own wells seem barren, it is a temporary emptiness.

When we reach our dippers in, the well of the collective unconscious is available.

Imagination's Truth

The imagination: is it a function of brain alone or of body too? Medical researcher and Nobel Prize winner Sir Peter Medawar says, in his book *Advice to a Young Scientist*, "Every discovery, every enlargement of the understanding begins as an imaginative preconception of what the truth might be." So, imagination is a leap of faith. We enter the unknown through it. And the poet William Carlos Williams believed that "Only the imagination is real." What of the soul? Isn't the imagination informed by faith and the soul's knowledge of the world? Imagination has a wild and liberating way of knowing, as does the soul. Sometimes I think imagination is more a function of soul than mind, that my imagination lives in my soul. Author Thomas Moore writes, "Imagination is always an increase of soul." Sometimes, when writing, you can actually feel that increase; the space in the body and the space in the room get larger. There's more there than before: more attention, more contrast, more feeling, a deeper sense of God's presence.

Through the imagination connections can be made that are daring, impossible, and true. What doesn't begin there? Before something can exist, we need to be able to imagine it, to attempt to make it true by imagining it. If we can't hold a thing in our imagination, how can we know it? In writing. Through writing, we initiate the process of making matter out of nonmatter. To take the leap of trusting the imagination requires faith. Without faith, what we imagine will remain flat and lifeless. Without imagination, there is nothing in which to have faith. Belief would be lost without it.

Faith and imagination are two invisibles. The poet Marvin Bell told me, "Since spirituality is nourished by imagination, perhaps they are twins." Your imagination will show you what you do and do not have faith in. If you follow the lead of the imagination, you can't know where you'll end up. I think of the Thule Eskimo poem by Nalungiaq that was collected by Knud Rasmussen sometime between 1921 and 1924. The Thule are the ancestors of the modern Inuit people.

In the earliest time,
when both people and animals lived on earth,
a person could become an animal if he wanted to
and an animal could become a human being.
Sometimes they were people
and sometimes animals
and there was no difference.
All spoke the same language.
That was the time when words were like magic.
The human mind had mysterious powers.
A word spoken by chance
might have strange consequences.
It would suddenly come alive
and what people wanted to happen could happen—
all you had to do was say it.
Nobody can explain this:
That's just the way it was.

That may have been just how it was but that sure isn't how it is any longer, not for most of us anyway. At the Royal British Columbia Museum on Victoria Island, in Canada, there's a large display where a viewer can witness the transformation. The various animal carvings—bear, wolf, raven—speak with human voices and tell their stories. According to Richard Crandall in *Inuit Art: A History,* "It is known through the ethnographic record that animals such as the bear, bird, walrus, and seal were believed to be powerful spirit helpers. . . . Carvings of the human-seal or human-bear forms may be associated with the ability of a shaman to transform into an animal spirit helper or enlist the use of a spirit helper to travel to the spirit world." At the exhibit, you can see the veil between the worlds evaporate. What am I most, I wonder, bear or whale, fox or raven?

The human mind does have mysterious powers. When we create art from the spiritual self, the truth of this becomes more and more apparent. Our words can be a kind of magic. They do make things happen, every day, the saddest things and the most joyous. When we look at the symbols we make, we can find the magic in them, how one thing means another and links us to a greater knowing and to each other. One of the closest ways we come to it in everyday life is in our night dreams, where the impossible is commonplace and unquestionable. Out for tea with two friends, at one of those cafes where they let you be kidlike by providing paper tablecloths and small buckets of crayons, I draw a picture of the shadow outline that the window frame makes on the table, the bright sun coming deliciously into the room and onto us, cold from a walk along the ocean. I'm awfully tired and have a bad headache and give no conscious thought to my picture. But after I put the crayons back in the tub, one friend asks about the crossroads I have drawn. She wants to know about my having closed all but two ways out. She wants to know about the blackened circle at the middle of the cross. I have nothing to tell her, having been in an awake dream and drawn from that, though I like her questions. They make me squirm a little. I know there's something there, a story I don't understand. The next morning it almost finds its way onto paper but I pull myself away, don't want to look at my two ways out right now, don't want to fall into that black dot that I circled so forcefully with the black crayon. Sometimes we don't want to know. And there are days when the right thing is to accept that.

Emily Dickinson knew: "The Possible's slow fuse is lit / By the Imagination." The imagination knows something is possible though it does not yet exist. And it isn't hurried, either; it's not troubled by the pace of the possible. My friend Marion tells me she's a turtle these days. What's coming through her is in no hurry—poems, stories, paintings—though some days she's impatient for the bounty of imagination not yet at her doorstep. As long as a thing is possible, it is lit and the imagination is on fire. You're seeing what you can't quite see and hearing what's not yet quite sound. The imagination makes this possible. It invites you into what's yet to be.

METAPHOR AND THE PLACE ITSELF

When writing, we live within images and metaphors. They're the symbols of the soul. In the imaginal worlds, the soul is most at home. The soul "thinks" in pictures. In response to my questions about the residence of the self, my student Ira Schiller composed the following poem:

> *The big red dot is not St. Louis.*
> *The small blue one is not Jamestown.*
> *Thin black lines are not Route 66.*
> *Nor is the double blue line I-5.*
> *And ascending topographic lines do not make you gasp for air.*
> *The curve of the rib is not the chest.*
> *The fold of the abdomen is not the belly.*
> *The angle of the shoulder is not the torso. . . .*

Metaphors illuminate the invisible, concretizing it and bringing it closer. They give us a way to talk about what can't be talked about any other way. An image can give an intimate vision and bring something up from the hidden self. To make a picture of something with words gives us the bridge from known to unknown, bringing the unknown closer, giving our imaginations something to play and live with.

In his book *Ariadne's Clue: A Guide to the Symbols of Humankind*, Anthony Stevens writes, "We possess an innate symbol forming propensity which exists as a healthy, creative, and integral part of our total psychic equipment." Much of what *Writing and the Spiritual Life* is about is recognizing and developing a relationship with the symbols we live with. By doing so, we may grow from their wisdom and bring their richness into our writing. It's part of the process of engaging the spiritual imagination. If you can visualize aspects of your inner world, your past, and the larger world to find the symbols, you'll increase your awareness of the meaning that exists for you in those places.

RECLAIMING THE CHILD'S AWARENESS

Within adults, the young child's way of being in the world and knowing it resides. I'm not speaking of adults' memories of what they did as children but the actual way their child-selves experienced reality. Within us, at greater or lesser degrees beneath the surface, this way of knowing is still intact. Part of the purpose of this chapter is to support your reclamation of it.

Young children's relationship with the world is multisensory. A child attends to how the wind feels against his cheek with a quality of attention that moves into the wind and the face and the touch. An adult may feel the same wind on her cheek, but before she can fully enjoy the experience, she's thinking about the clothes out on the line, hoping the wind won't be so strong as to snap them off. We often remove ourselves from primary, unquestioned, or unanalyzed awareness. Or it has been educated out of us. Our years of living have influenced it. Of course, education and our daily lives also enlarge the base of our ways of knowing. I'm not suggesting you discount all that, but I am suggesting you develop a way of knowing that's direct and simultaneously physical, emotional, spiritual, and intellectual, a way that is inclusive of adulthood and childhood realities.

Poetry meets me where I live, and it can express reality in the way I truly know and embody it. Many hours of my childhood were spent with poetry. I got to know and understand myself and the world through poems. I felt part of a conversation. Poems spoke to and within me. I spoke back. Growing up at my house, I had to prove points in clear, succinct sentences with only a limited amount of time to do so. The kitchen clock was ticking. I'd stumble and forget what I knew. My middle childhood through young adulthood was spent trying to know the way my father and teachers taught me to know. It wasn't based on intuitive knowing or the imagination or self-trust but on the theory that the child is the empty cup and the adults and books are there to fill her up. I didn't want to be filled. I wanted to be. To know through being is different than to know through being filled with information. As a child I didn't want information. I wanted the way the light came in and what my dolls thought of it. I wanted the echo of our voices, my mother's and mine, through the tunnel and how I learned about sound and the meaning of repetition through those daily walks in the subway tunnel. I knew about darkness because I was both afraid in it and desired it. Vincent van Gogh said, "One of the most beautiful things one can do is to paint the darkness, which nonetheless has light in it." I wanted to paint the darkness and my fear of it, to find the light in it. My fear and desire weren't things I wanted to defend or justify. I didn't need to convince another of their veracity. It was a knowing of my spirit-self. I spoke to God. God and Mary and the angels spoke to me. Just as the trees talked and the whistling train talked. I didn't doubt myself as a young child. By being pushed from my spiritual self I was, in essence, taught to doubt myself. So I have spent these many years getting back. I'm not back all the way. It's like a wave, in and out and in again. When the sand sucks the water in, I think, what water? Certain things we know don't need to be supported by facts and proofs, diagrams and theories, but first we need to trust the knowing within us, the mind, body, soul, spirit, word, and heart. The proof may come later.

Young children know, without being conscious that they know, that awareness isn't a straight line. They don't rationalize and compartmentalize experience. There's more fluidity between dream, memory, thought, past, present, future, and the body. Children are less likely to analyze a situation by trying to decide if it's good or bad. If it's good, they smile, and if it's bad, they cry. They don't have an experience and say, "Well, that was my spiritual self being engaged." Children aren't trying hard to fit the experience into a category; they're just in it. Particularly for young children, those who haven't been mistreated, there's a greater acceptance of what happens. Mistreatment causes the self to fracture, to divide off and shut down.

The child's innate desire is to play and interact with the world around him. The connection between the child and the world is direct and joyous, unencumbered. An infant will play with her hand, watching the shapes it makes in the air. Play implies freedom and invention. A child will use language playfully as well. Young children are true poets of meaning, sound, and rhythm.

ALL YOU'VE EVER KNOWN

Within you there's the self who knows the world in more ways than one all at the same time, who possesses simultaneous awareness of shadow and light, past and present. To connect back with that self is to connect with the essential self, the spirited and spiritual being you are. By reacquainting yourself with your initial ways of experiencing the world, you may find that barriers break down between concepts and feeling, past and present, right and wrong. You may find bonds within that are imagistic, spiritual, and emotional in nature. Memories exist in your body of the early times and how you then responded to them. The poet Lucille Clifton reminds us, "this past was waiting for me / when i came." To call upon these memories can connect you to your spiritual self, to the earlier you who was free from doubting magic. If you write from this place, you'll find the voice of your spiritual nature takes on a dimension it didn't have before. You may write with an unfaltering acceptance of what comes. Your awareness of nuance, detail, the tremulous, and the half-hidden will increase. You're likely to make connections you hadn't considered before.

The poet Martha Collins said, "For me, at least, one aim of writing poetry, however unrealizable, is a reclamation of all the language I have ever known." To reclaim the language you have known—heard and spoken—is to connect with a wealth of, not only the language itself, but experience and voice. When writing authentically, you can welcome the entire self. Don't leave anything behind. What's yours is yours, and it's in your bag of goods, the parts you accept and the parts you scorn. If you try to leave part of yourself behind in the process, you will lose the essential link to the spiritual universe of which you are a part. Connection cannot be maintained if a part is cut off because the imagination and the soul get truncated. Sifting through the mind's material for what is acceptable to say is a form of self-censorship. Your inner world of spirit, which is linked to all spirits, won't throw any part of you out.

WRITING AND KNOWING

When we write from the inner, spiritual self, we employ an integration of our many ways of knowing. They come together to express what we're drawn to say. No one way of knowing takes precedence. There's a unity of consciousness that the soulful self trusts and believes in. Writing from a spiritual base is about staying open to the rational and the irrational, to the planned and the unplanned. It's about accepting guidance we might not cognitively understand. If we write from our home within, we begin in a secure spot and send our radar out in every direction. It's not at all a thoroughly planned organization; rather, it's random and sporadic, fast and then slow, backward and then forward. Images, thoughts, and reflections that seem to come from nowhere enter into our writing. They come from the mix of who we are, what and how we know. Around and around, language spins in our minds and we catch it like hungry fishermen.

The eyes inform the heart, and the intellect talks to the soul. Intuition takes its cues from every place. You sense what word comes next, and you trust that's right because you feel it to be so. You experience that "click" of rightness, like a key fitting snugly into a lock and the door opening. Your ways of knowing come together in the place where you live most deeply, the seat of awareness that we spoke of in the previous chapter.

When I'm writing, all my receptors are open to receive information like a tree that takes the wind, sun, and rain everywhere—on its leaves, branches, bark, and the core inside. The birds on the tree know the elements as well, and the tree knows them, their presence on its limbs. I'm attentive in every way possible. It's an opening prayer. All my ways of listening listen to each other. And isn't this how we know

God or the Great Spirit—through the open boat of a ready heart?
With my ears I can hear more than the actual. The spiritual self relies
on and has faith in all our ways of knowing. The richest work will
come from that unity of being, a receptive yet pointed awareness. The
paper will hold your truths. They won't blow away or disappear like
a night dream too soon forgotten.

For the Notebook 1

"EVERY FIBER TOLD"

memory demands so much,
it wants every fiber
told and retold

DENISE LEVERTOV, from *This Great Unknowing: Last Poems*

For all the years of your life there are memories. They're
tucked and stacked away inside. Find a quiet, comfortable
spot where you won't be disturbed for an hour or so. Rather
than calling a memory up, you might try the following process. Read this exercise through first, and then begin.

Rest your body, relax, and breathe. Notice how you feel.
Take note of the room you're sitting in, the quality of light,
sounds in the background. You might close your eyes and ease
yourself back to an early memory and focus, not so much on
the event itself, but on its sensory nature. Notice where in your
body you remember what happened. Do you know it in your
feet, through the tunnel of your ears? Without trying to understand your response, take note of the first words that come to
you to describe that memory. Accept them and write them
down. What are the pieces of the memory that call to you?
What's the next spontaneous thing to follow? What you will
find on the paper isn't the memory itself. First you have an

experience. Then it transforms into memory. Writing it down changes it. There's the experience you have while writing and then there is the poem or story. What's on the paper will be a new thing. It will include the influence of all that's transpired since the event you recalled, the ways in which you and the world have changed. And then if you share the poem or story with others, they won't have your memory and they won't have your writing, they'll have their own thing inspired by your words.

Spend an hour visualizing and then writing. Be sure to take a few minutes to read back to yourself what you've written.

For the Notebook 2

What the Body Knows

Right there where you're sitting now, look at your hands. What do they perceive? Do your fingers know best their coolness at this moment? What can they tell you? Do they have words for your paper? What do your ears know? What do they hear that's far from you and what do they hear that's close? Attend to your body, to wherever your attention is drawn, and write down what you notice—what you see, hear, smell, or intuit. If your hand could talk, what would it say? If your shoulder could listen, what would it hear? This is a practice of receiving what's there, gathering the body's knowing into your world of words. The body has a history to tell you if you'll stop and take note. You can apply this process to any area of your body: blood and muscle, knees and lungs.

See what fifteen minutes of writing will give you. This is a good exercise to return to at moments when you want to write but aren't sure what to say. You may find this writing exercise easily leads you into your next subject.

CHAPTER 3

THE CALLING VOICE
AND STORYTELLING

*Herein dwells the still small voice to which
my spiritual self is attuned.*

Mary McLeod Bethune

*A butterfly lights on the branch
Of your green voice.*

James Wright, *from* The Branch Will Not Break

*Wake up, you poets:
let echoes end,
and voices begin.*

Antonio Machado, *from* Times Alone:
Selected Poems of Antonio Machado

In 1986, the Michigan State Legislature declared Aretha Franklin's voice to be one of the state's natural resources. What a concept! The voice as a resource. A country's resources are its wealth, "its means of producing wealth," according to my dictionary. Franklin's voice is a spiritual resource. Every time I hear her sing, I know why. Her voice is robust and beautiful. She slips into the low places, strong and steady there, then rises up to loftier notes. Hearing her sing, I want to live in her voice because it seems to say, "You're going to encounter the difficult but you're going to come out OK." And, her voice says, stay with me awhile as I sing to you: loss, regret, joy, and the presence of the holy. Her voice can also be spunky—moving fast from one sound to the next, it energizes me. When I've got a difficult job to do, I turn her music on. When there's a long drive ahead, it's her tape I put into the player. I sing along and make the car shake. When confidence is lagging, she reminds me to respect myself. Her voice resonates with fortitude and strength, harmony and melody. Franklin's voice speaks to me in the place where I live.

Your voice is your own natural resource. Its worth in your life and the lives of others may match the birds' need for sky. Unsung, your voice would remain trapped under your breath, which is like no voice at all, because it would remain invisible and unknown. When we're silent but the need to speak our necessary truths is burgeoning, we risk illness of the soul, mind, and body. And the wisdom of the self may go underground. It's always a risk to write and speak your truth, but the risk of not doing so is greater. You have only to speak with your own voice, in its rhythms, with its melody and cadence, the voice right there within you, your distinctly human voice. In her Nobel Prize acceptance speech in 1993, Toni Morrison said, "Wordwork is sublime because it is generative. It makes meaning that secures our difference, our human difference, the way in which we are like no other life." That generative quality can come through the voice, *your* voice. I can almost hear it, even from this distance.

You can't fully know the value of your voice and its message until you sing. While standing outside a house, even if you peek in through the uncurtained windows, you can't know how it would feel to be in those rooms. From the outside you can't know if the air is fresh or stale. You can't know the softness of that green chair in the living room. Nor can you know the mood moving between the people who live there. You may guess, but you won't know. When you begin to speak from your deepest self and write in your own voice—not the voice you thought maybe you should have, but that which is uniquely yours—the gate to the speaking opens wider and wider. You'll find the wealth of your own worth in the singing.

Writing in your true voice shortens the divide between self and soul, self and other, self and world. Your spiritual self may initiate a new kind of conversation, one that's personal and intimate, one that accepts the unacceptable, one that lets the unknown in, one that welcomes grace, one that's political and global and possesses a knowing that extends beyond your own doorstep. A Wallace Stevens poem says, "She had no world of her own / Except the one she sang and singing, made." Singing brings the world into view. By stating the truth, claiming it, the voice can make things happen. It may give you a world you didn't have before. The poet Elizabeth Spires writes, "Poetry . . . holds a mirror to the world." It may direct you toward unexplored territory: a view of the iced-over lake or that clutch of mountains turning orange in the fading light which you'd never seen till now; words you'd never thought of using come in quick succession. Your awareness becomes more precise and detailed. With the force of breath or the indelibility of ink, perceptions shift, expand, and focus. The words bring certain details closer, give them form. When you write, the paper holds the manifestation of your voice and steadies it there, which allows you to see things with a bit of distance. Through writing you can gain clarity and new meaning. Words can make things happen. The Native American poet N. Scott Momaday said, "People in the Anglo-Saxon period, for example, uttered charms over their fields so that the seeds would grow into harvest. They believed that they could bring that about by exercising the power of the voice; they could affect physical change in the world. Now, that is believing in language! And that's the way I want to believe in it. That's the way the American Indian has traditionally believed in it." What kind of belief will you put into what you have to say? Belief and language make an alchemy that occurs when the spiritual self is expressed through writing. If you are willing to regard truth, your own truth, as necessary and believable, you may have to follow sentence upon sentence, and what may come is an unraveling of how you thought things were. The risk in writing our truths is that our ways of knowing and being may have to broaden to accommodate new awarenesses. But in the process, we'll discover the many stories that dwell within us and their wisdom.

YOUR SPIRITUAL VOICE

In the Gospel according to Saint John, it is written, "In the beginning was the Word, and the Word was with God, and the Word was God." Out of nothing came something, and it was the word of God. The word, the voice, is the breath of life. Inspiration has its root in breath: to inspire is to breathe, to inhale and exhale life. Your strongest voice is your most truthful, spiritual voice. It's the voice of your essential self. Your breath sustains it. When you write from your spiritual depth, your innermost source, you can access this voice. The more you listen, the more this part of you will speak, whatever topic you're writing about. Give yourself the opportunity to develop and speak with it. Its wisdom is greater than you might anticipate.

This voice lies underneath the "Hi, how are you?" voice. It is deeper than doubt and hesitation. Your greatest knowing will be spoken with your spiritual voice. It exists at the foundation of who you are. The spiritual voice is primary, and it connects you to the essence in all things. This voice has the quality of the imperative and speaks what must be spoken. It can be trusted.

When I'm writing from my spiritual self, the words nearly write themselves; I'm driven by them and feel myself carried by the impulse behind the writing. Whatever obstacles I may have felt before sitting down—such as "I can't write this. It's too big" or "I have one sentence but no idea what comes next"—have evaporated. The words come through despite myself. Sometimes I have layers of curtains to move past to arrive at my authenticity, but it's there and I get to it eventually. The spiritual voice comes out of love. Love dwells there. I feel cared for. I'm graced with the divinity that connects us all.

Our spiritual voices are made up of the mix of who we are and all we've been and done, who we were as children, who we are as adults. When I speak of the spiritual voice, I'm not just referring to one way of speaking or any particular subject matter. One's most true voice is about a quality of expression that is genuine and heartfelt. From it comes authentic expression. This voice will not lie.

FINDING YOUR WRITER'S VOICE

Over many years of teaching I've found that for a lot of people there's a divide between their desire to write authentically and daringly and their confidence or willingness to risk doing so. The urge to speak— and by speaking I mean in a large sense, inclusive of the act of writing—is itself unfettered and pure, but the voice may be hidden under years of silence. If you've spent a long time not tending to what you're called to say, the desire may have gotten blocked. Fear of the unknown will hold a voice under wraps, with a fear of breaking rules coming close behind. To locate your voice, you may first have to find out if anything stops it from coming forward. Does something hold you back? Has it been snatched or lost, or have you just not recognized its need to be spoken? Or is your voice free and unfettered?

Novelist Maxine Hong Kingston said, "You see everybody . . . has the same struggle to break through taboos, to find your voice." There's the family taboo, cultural and gender taboos, the religious taboo, and more. If we're to speak authentically, we've got to see those hindrances for what they are, acknowledge them, and move past what holds us back. Or maybe it's a matter of moving into. As Robert Frost wrote, "The best way out is always through." I've found that breathroughs aren't accomplished by force. Rather, bring the taboos against speaking with you and speak anyway, speak to them and for them. Ignoring the inner "no" can shut down the self and the essence of the self, the soul. To deny the "no" is to deny all that got you to where you are today and all that holds you back. Those taboos may have been introduced to us a long time ago and are nearly brothers. Say, "I see you" to the "no" and watch it change its stance.

From when I was young, my father, teachers, and, somewhat, my mother doubted the value, veracity, and intellect behind the expression of my thoughts. I incorporated that doubt and chose, except when I felt really comfortable, to hide. I wanted to be approved of, to do things right, but because my responses, the deductions I made, and my awarenesses were often not regarded as "right" or "true," I hid my voice, as though to protect something tender. And yet I had things to say, wanted to speak, and was driven to write.

To get to the speaking, you must uncover your voice. If there's a weight holding it down, lift it up. And that calls for faith, faith that the words will come, faith that you will be guided toward the saying, faith in your greater knowing, and faith in the presence of God or the Great Spirit guiding you. In this case, faith becomes a very active, moving force. It flickers and shines like light. You take your faith and urge it into words.

You don't have to know what you want to write. You don't have to believe in your voice, in what you will say, or how you might say it. It begins with the impulse and craving to say. Desire, a wedge of it, and faith are what's needed. You feel called to the page. And there's your first word, the first phrase, which becomes the story's first sentence and is followed by the next sentence. Curiosity will carry you a long way, as will the tenacity to stay with the process over bumps and into dark alleys. Some writers consider writing a need that's as basic as many others and more than some, a way to know the world. Psychologist Helen Resneck, who wrote a book about her family's experience when her father became ill with Alzheimer's, says, "The only way I feel known is through writing. It's my voice that gets me inside and then to the other side of an experience."

Susan, a woman who's been in an ongoing writing workshop with me for the past few years, sent me a note after a recent class: "That writing Thursday night was a real breakthrough for me. Finally saying those feelings to others reduced their power—the world didn't end! As I bared my soul, I saw acceptance and understanding in the eyes of you beautiful women." She had her say and it didn't cause things to fall apart; in fact, she felt affirmed. It is always a risk to write and read one's truth, but the risk of not doing so is greater.

There's a way that voice is uncontainable. It wants to be spoken, and speaking it connects us with our deepest knowing, whether it's an urgently written journal entry or a call for justice that insists we speak out and not accept the status quo. What do you dream of saying? What truth would you scale mountains for? What lie are you intent on uncovering? What have you known forever but never said? What do you believe despite what anyone has told you otherwise? What question do you want to ask, and who do you hope will answer it?

You'll find your voice in what you dream, in what you have faith in, in what you long for. A friend of mine tells me that for years she's had a recurring dream. "I'm standing, nowhere in particular, trying to walk forward, but it's impossible to get anywhere. It takes enormous effort to lift my leg in order to take a step. I can't do it. It's like I'm in sand or mud. I can't move. I'm caught struggling against it." I suggested she write into the dream to discover what it was trying to say to her. What do her legs have to say? And where's she trying to get to that's so impossible? What's the message that craves being spoken, the voice of the dream? The dream repeats until we finally stop and listen to what it has to say. When she looked closely and wrote into the dream, she realized that she was trying to get somewhere new in her life but was feeling held back.

Sources of Voice

When we write in our most authentic voices, we draw from many sources simultaneously. Our individual voices are a unique combination of many things. Family, neighborhood, region, gender, ethnicity, class, social history, and personal circumstance are all encoded in who we are and how we'll speak. How you were spoken to as a child at the dinner table and how you responded will influence how you speak now. The atmosphere around your learning to write as a child will influence how you feel about writing. There are layers and layers to experience. You are not separate from the culture or the environment when you write. These lineages contribute to making your writing what it is. It's not as if they're static, and neither is your interpretation or response. Your view of the past is contingent upon many things, including your knowledge of it, your personal awareness, your need. There's a relationship at work, and it is reciprocal. Your writing is determined by what's happened. We communicate with our voices, and they are a social tool as well as a tool for self-discovery. My friend the writing professor says, "I'm compelled to write when someone says, 'We need your help. Would you write about this issue facing the school board now?'" The future may be influenced by your words.

A VOICE TO LISTEN FOR
The Writer's Calling

It's not like the phone rings and the voice on the other end says, "Hey, Charlie, have I got a poem for you!" But it is like that. Only the phone doesn't ring. Your head rings. It's buzzing. My student Liz wrote, "I had to stop the car to get the poem. It would have vanished if I hadn't pulled over, and I was in a hurry to pick up the kids and the rain was just pounding down. But none of that mattered for the moment, only what I might be able to say."

The writer's calling is that large sense of voice that compels you to write. It may stop you in your tracks and insist on being heard. Mystics are called to follow their paths. And you may be as well. For some writers, that calling manifests as a voice they listen for when they're writing. The poet Grace Schulman describes her process: "I hear lines, words, images, the muses of the line. I take notes sometimes

so I won't forget. Once I dreamed a haiku in exactly seventeen syllables. I wake up with poetry in my head."

When you take up the call as a writer, you follow the voice into
written language. The drive to write may be undeniable, coming at any
time of day, whether you're prepared or not. You wake to it and sleep
in it. Though it may be absent at times, it returns. Lines come rushing in, and you feel required to write them. You're curious. You're
taken. It's falling in love. My friend, the poet Maude Meehan, just
called. She was excited. "Yesterday I wrote the first poem I have written in a long time. I thought that maybe the little stroke last year had
shut off that part of my brain. But no, there I was at the kitchen sink
when this idea came. I was still in my nightie. I took my rubber gloves
off, left the dirty dishes as they were, and sat down to write what I
heard."

So, for as much as writing is an act of expression, it's also an act
of awareness, of listening. Listening is a receptive activity. The more
you listen to the call, the more you are called to listen, to attend to
the material that is right there at your feet, to offer your awareness to
that. It's the traffic jam, the morning news, the birds on the wire. It's
the neighbor's eighteen-year-old deaf cat who dies late Friday night,
having been hit by a car, and you think, "What a lousy way to go for
someone who's quietly walked the streets so many years." If you alert
your antenna, you will become a conduit for what's out there and
what's in there. There is so much to hear.

When you were a child, did your mother call you for dinner from
your outdoor play in the evenings in the middle of the hot summer?
Can you remember the instant you recognized it was her voice, not
your friend's mother, not some vague mumbling that you could continue to ignore? Though you wouldn't want to leave your game and
your friends so soon, you'd scurry home, realizing you were hungry,
knowing you'd better get going. That moment of recognition becomes
fine-tuned in a spiritual writing practice. In one way or another, I'm
always listening, though the days I listened for my mother's voice
are long gone. The voice that calls the writer isn't calling you away

from something but into it. Of course, there are times we choose not to listen. Unfortunately, we can't always say, "Hey, wait up; now I'm ready." The voice that calls us to the page isn't always as intent on getting us to listen as our mothers were on getting us to dinner. So it's up to you to take the invitation or give your regrets, risking the chance that days or even weeks may go by before the voice comes calling for you again.

In *Letters to a Young Poet*, Rainer Maria Rilke wrote, "Ask yourself in the most silent hour of your night: *must* I write? Dig into yourself for a deep answer. And if this answer rings out in assent, if you meet this solemn question with a strong, simple '*I must*,' then build your life in accordance with this necessity; your whole life, even into its humblest and most indifferent hour, must become a sign and witness to this impulse."

How you build a "life in accordance with this necessity" has more to do with what goes on within you than without. It has to do with awareness and attention. Paying attention is an expression of gratitude for what you've been given, a way to honor life's richness and complexity. This can be done anywhere, anytime. But it also means that you make a place and time to respond to the calling.

A Quiet Calling

The call may be a rather shyly offered invitation. You probably won't be picked up by the shirt collar and carried to a desk, and told, "Now write." Do you think that a calling is for someone other than you, that you aren't one of the chosen? Do you feel reluctant to pick up a pen and easily talk yourself out of what you consider to be just a slight inclination? To be called doesn't necessarily mean words pour into your ears and drown out the voices of your loved ones with their insistence and beauty. The writer's call may be more subtle than that. Rilke's mandate may be overshadowed for you by daily responsibilities. To be called just means you want to follow an ineffable something into language, that you are moved to do so.

Not all who are called will choose to devote their entire lives to writing. The spiritual writing life doesn't require that. After having dug deep, maybe writing's just one of the things that ignites your creativity and your soul. And, at that, it may be supplanted by things like child rearing and making a living. There's not just one way to write, spiritually or otherwise. There's the way that *you* respond and find language, a way that meets your need for expression, for turning written language into something more vibrant and taut than "to do" lists. The important thing is that you respond and take notice, not how often and at what time of day.

If you make a space to listen for the words, they'll show up. Over time, there will be ever more of them. A voice becomes available to you that wasn't before. If you take the position of asking questions, there's always another question following on the heels of the one you're writing down and answering.

What Calls to You?

Hildegard Von Bingen, the eleventh-century nun and mystic, said, "I heard a voice from heaven saying . . . write what you see and hear." Clearly, she felt directed. What you see and hear won't be what your sister or father sees and hears, not what your best friend will write. And you can't entirely anticipate what it will be. What calls you to write will be specific to who you are. It will take you into new language. It's a powerful experience. The capacity of the imagination is endless.

Years ago I was at a writing conference when a well-known writer posed the following question to a large group of students present for her lecture. "Say a poet is toward the end of his career; he'll write, maybe, just one more book. What should its focus be?" I squirmed in my seat at the absurdity of the question and because I felt we were being set up. There was a correct answer in the mind of the teacher. I knew not to raise my hand, because my answer was not the one she was after. My answer would have been that this elderly writer should write what was in his heart to write and that he wouldn't know what that was until he put pen to paper. The poet leading the discussion was pleased to explain the "correct" answer, although no one in the audience quite got it: "The poet should write a final book that is political in nature. He should champion the cause of the natural world. With his stature, this is his obligation." But what if he's not called in that direction? Certainly we can be directed toward our subject, toward our calling. Why we may be drawn to write about certain things in particular ways may be mysterious, but it's not only mysterious. We write about what we care for, what we think needs to be said for various reasons. The direction of our work is based on inspirations that come from the outside and the inside. Political and environmental needs can make for callings, if that's what we're drawn to. The spiritual can exist there as well.

If I were to impose a direction on myself that was not in line with my larger knowing, that was not authentic to my calling, my voice would be silent. The job of the writer is to stay open to what calls, "to keep the channel open," as Martha Graham said in regard to dance. If the channel remains open, what needs to come through will. The poet N. Scott Momaday said, "To be a Kiowa is to have a subject— but then everybody can say that about his experience, whatever it happens to be."

YOUR VOICE ON PAPER

The writer's voice engaged in writing isn't quite the same as the one that has been whispering to him. The calling voice opens the writer into the place within, calls him to recognize it. He hears something and it becomes him, as though the words are channeled through him. It may be an event close by and personal or something far away that calls him to write a certain poem or story. He may want to use his voice to respond to another. A writer doesn't necessarily have just one writing voice, but various voices depending on what he's writing. Each text has its particular voice; a particular style will be authentic to the writing while another won't. The voice of a mythic poem isn't going to be the same as the voice of an essay about the garden and its rows of foxglove newly in bloom. The sound and pacing will not be the same, to say nothing of the content. Many things come into play. Purpose, mood, subject, and audience all contribute to how the voice is expressed on paper.

Novelists talk about hearing the various voices of a novel's characters. Once you find the voice of the piece, the whole of the story may become clear. It's as though the story needed its voice to have an identity.

Doris Lessing said:

> *I think that the difficulty, when you're writing, is to find what I call the tone of voice.* That is, the appropriate way for this particular book or story. It might take a long time to get that right. . . . For example, *The Marriages Between Zones Three, Four, and Five*—I had that in my mind for about ten years, but I simply couldn't think of a way to do it. And when I thought of using that ancient device as storyteller, suddenly it came into place—the tone of the book, everything. Not just like that; it *did* take me a long time to do it, you know. . . .

The content of what you write will not be what it would have been in conversation. The way voice manifests through writing is distinctly different from speech. When you're writing, there is no immediate other, and what you give to the page is greatly affected by this. There's more space around not only the actual language, but the ideas. If you're writing, you can go back later and edit. Not so in conversation, even though you can recant. And the rhythms of writing are their own. The cadence of your spoken voice has sound, and its pace may change depending on the conversation. Writing also has cadence and pacing, but they aren't directly affected by the social structure of conversation. There's more time in writing to spread out, and what you listen for is more ephemeral than another person's voice speaking to you. This is particularly true about an open-ended, non-deadline-based kind of writing, a writing that exists in the present tense, yet embraces the past and—less centrally—the future. To give the written voice this kind of room allows the voice its say, even if you intend the piece of writing to move out of the notebook and into the world. Start here first, with this kind of room for your voice.

What the Paper Holds

The written voice remains on the paper and is less transitory than the spoken voice, which, for the most part, is here and gone. We may be willing to say something fleetingly that we might not say if it had the potential of longevity. I'll write a number of things down if I believe no one else will read them, but when I'm planning for the work to go beyond me, I'll choose my words in a manner particular to my audience, purpose, and so on. When writing, no matter what, you are always your own first audience. If you keep in mind that you, the writer, will choose what and when the work goes past you into the world, it may free you to write what you might otherwise hesitate to. It's only from that point of willingness and openness that you get to your greatest material. Where the work goes after it's down on paper and how it gets revised is up to you.

After the words are down on the paper and you've read the piece aloud a few times for the sound of the words, to know whether they fulfill their purpose, tranquility often follows. You've met your mark. It's like having eaten a feast; you need nothing but to recognize your hunger's gone. For now, the saying has been said.

THE SPOKEN VOICE

The spoken voice can hold your longing. Its sound may say what your words don't. It may give you away at times and unwittingly show your hand to the crowd. Your voice may redeem you. Its sound can make you change your mind.

Speaking connects self with sound, with breath, with heartbeat, with soul, with the other. Writing with pen and paper is a way of speaking. When you add the dimension of sound, a larger thing can happen. Voice enters the empty space. You take what is intimate, because it is your own—both content and sound—and let it go.

After writing, or in the midst of a day's work, many writers will read the new material aloud to themselves. When you hear your words you know them better and can listen for what's missing or what's been overstated. When I read work in progress aloud, I can hear what wasn't apparent in the act of writing or even reading it silently. I hear myself speak, yes, but that original voice, the one that called me to the writing in the first place, comes through too. Reading the work out loud can help you recognize the tone of the piece and an authority you may not have known it had. Reading your work out loud can also be seductive. Your tone of voice, your sense of when to pause, may allow you to read more sympathetically than your readers, and that may deceive you into not revising the work. If the writing's going to serve any kind of public purpose, it's important to be aware that it needs to stand alone, without your voice to fill in the missing pieces.

The voice can carry you into public in a powerful way. You stand before an audience and read the words you've spent hours or days on in order to get them just right. When the voice joins together with the intention of the writing and the time put into it, an audience can tell. You may be stilled into listening. It's helpful to recognize the power of the voice before getting up in front of a crowd. I coordinated a series of poetry and prose readings for many years and remember one time a writer got up to read a story. But she couldn't do it. The story of the piece was still tied to her. She was still such a part of the words, so inside them, that she cried while reading. At first there were only a few tears. Then a flood. It was a truly sad story about a girl who had witnessed her father's death. This writer had never read the piece out loud before, not to a friend, not even to herself. For a few moments she couldn't speak, and it was as though the audience held its collective breath waiting for her. The poignancy of her expression brought the group together. Her crying slowly subsided and, with tissue in hand and a smattering of tears, she read to us.

HOUSEHOLD REMINDERS

We often need reminders so that we don't stride along in the old, comfortable way, unconsciously renouncing the voice's need to speak. Maybe you need to announce it, to yourself anyway, and put up imaginary road signs: "Twenty miles ahead, natural resource: Mark's voice." A billboard with shiny red letters that reads, "Coming up on your left, Sarah's mellifluous voice." Or display real notes around your house to remind you that you have something to say. At times, I've pasted little messages on the bathroom mirror, above the refrigerator door handle, or on top of the coffeepot: "Is there something you've been meaning to say?" Or your list of things to do: "Water plants, walk dog, write." Not a bad thing to do after walking the dog! Better yet: "Write, walk dog, water plants." First things first. Sometimes just the word *poetry* in bold, block letters posted in strategic spots around the house is enough to remind me of what I love so much. Sad that I often let bill paying and lesson planning and dinner cooking take precedence; it's still a challenge, after more than twenty years of writing, to put my voice first, especially when the written words don't provide me with immediate rewards—either financial or of apparent value to others. It's difficult to put my voice first when I'm fearful of what I might write down. Writing those fears doesn't necessarily make them go away, but now I see them more clearly for what they are, and I don't sign on their dotted line. I don't say, "Fear of failure, I will bow to you and keep my lips sealed and my fingers crossed." Rather, it's, "Oh, there you are, fear. Have a seat; here's some tea."

I have to remind myself that the subtle benefits of writing and giving voice to the deep stuff are what keep me whole and alive and able to perform all the other necessary, outward-bound duties with love in my heart. Writing keeps me spiritually, at least somewhat, intact. I bring my *unintactness* to the writing and lay it on the page. The work of writing carries me a great distance. It heals many ills, but it isn't a one-size-fits-all life preserver. Writing is one of the relationships I

have. There's work—spiritual, emotional, political, interpersonal—
that it can't do. It can lead me to where I need to go, direct me toward
what I've got to do. The fact that it keeps my voice resonant, flexible,
and unstuck is a big thing.

SUPPORT FOR YOUR VOICE

Writing is a way to sustain and nurture friendships. It's a way to
respond. We need to remind each other of our voices and the places
they hold in our lives and memory.

In yesterday's mail along with the usual boring envelopes was a
picture postcard of Prague from my friend Gabriella with a note that
said, in its entirety, "Hope you're writing a poem today!" She signed
it, "Much love, soul comadre, Gabi." I thought of her voice and her
poems, the one about when she was a young woman, living for the first
time far away from her mother, and how both of them would go out
to Kentucky Fried Chicken on the same day, at the same hour, order
the same meal, and eat dinner, basking, even with a separation the
length of California, in each other's love. After I got her card, I sat
down and wrote this paragraph instead of a poem, comforted and
happy, imagining Gabriella at her desk writing too, working on poems
or her dissertation. I liked feeling her presence as I wrote. It helped
increase my faith in the writing. I keep Gabriella's fried chicken poem
with me, and when I'm hungry, I take a bite and am filled, my fingers
pleasantly greasy!

To speak with your soul-voice you don't need complicated equipment; there are no gizmos with attachable pieces to connect, no elab-
orate instructions. You need pen, paper, a little time, and a discovery
frame of mind. Consider yourself the explorer of your voice. No one
can tell you how your voice should sound.

The things that support your spiritual life will also support your
voice. Poetry, nature, solitude, and friends support mine, not always
in that order. When I read certain poems, they're proof to me of
imminent nature, majesty, and spiritual knowing. Poetry reminds me

of deepest truth and that unexpected things happen there. Linda Gregg, in her poem "Sometimes," writes, "The soul makes out of ashes, / out of quicklime and white walls, / a crowd of seraphim singing." I am touched in that primary, ephemeral spot, where my spiritual voice comes from, and that part of me is rekindled. The voice comes from where I live, that inner home we talked about earlier.

LETTING YOUR VOICE TELL THE STORIES

The poet Sonia Sanchez said, "We are in danger, great danger of losing the memory that connects us, that keeps us alive." If we don't tell our stories and listen to the stories of others, they will get lost. And if the memories get lost, parts of our spirit go with them. Storytelling—whether spoken or written, as poems or prose—isn't something we need permission to do, and yet, in the hustle and bustle of our days, it's as if we do. We often don't make enough time for our stories to be welcomed as integral parts of each other's lives. I'm talking about the more than superficial tales that you don't know the last words of until you tell them while making conversation out of the fiber of your life. The meaning of a particular encounter needs the question only a friend can ask, and this doesn't fit into sound-byte fragments of time. It needs to spread out to take wing. My friend and longtime student Darrie says, "I am tired of the appearance of listening." That look, we all know it, when someone nods his head up and down and you think he might as well be nodding off for all the true listening that's going on. I think we pull away from honest listening when we're living lives that leave us frayed, when we too have such a call to be listened to. We need to share our stories to discover and then integrate their significance and for personal and cultural change to take place. Through telling and listening, we become more a part of each other, and we can move the stories out of the small "me" into the large "me," the "usness" of the collective.

After a 7.1 earthquake hit the San Francisco and Monterey Bay areas, our local bookstore asked for members of the community to help them pack and move books out of their building which had been declared unsafe and would soon be torn down. The bookshop's staff anticipated that a small group of people would show up and were taken by surprise when more than four hundred of us did. That day hundreds of "Where were you at 5:04 P.M. on October 17th?" stories were traded while we dusted and hoisted the store's wealth of books. Weeks later a number of local writers gave a reading that was held at the high school. Not all the poets and writers read earthquake pieces, but we read our lives to each other and came together intimately in a kind of solidarity. I don't remember a time when the community felt closer. It lasted a good long while too. Maybe, ten years later, we're still feeling it, a little. The story got larger. It was our shared story. It had to be told. Nothing could take us away from it.

A number of readily available distractions can pull us away from ourselves and each other, from the stories of our lives. If kids are having supper in front of computer screens and parents are forgoing dinner for evening meetings and we don't have cataclysmic events that insist we hear their stories, where are the stories of our regular days and what happens to them? It seems we're bent on reaching out for the external "more and better" and have let slip the need to reach in to the stories of our friendships. If we fill our lives with constant activity, when do we make time for the intimate unfolding, layer by layer, detail by just-realized detail, to be told and held in some kind of intimate community?

The stories go underground and disappear in the next day's activities and those stories, and so on. But by listening to and telling our stories, we know who we are as individuals, as families, as communities. The stories make us who we are, illuminate our perceptions of the world, define what we care about, bring us to the heart of what each other's struggles are.

There's talk about the rise of breast cancer among women in northern and central California. Some physicians say there are more incidents of it. Others say it just looks that way because more women in these areas are attentive to the potential problem and are more likely to identify the disease through early diagnosis and reporting. This dispute makes the papers every now and then. I know more women than I can count on both hands who've had breast cancer. Most have survived, but not all have. My friend, the writer Lynn Luria Sukenick, is no longer here. I miss her words—spoken and on paper. My friend Amy Cooperstein, with whom I taught for many years, is gone. Diana is well, teaching less than full-time this year, her two children now grown and in college. Wendy, too, is strong and newly a mother.

When my friend Janet's mammogram was abnormal and showed a sudden display of calcium deposits, I was alarmed and braced myself for the worst. She visited; we talked about options and the arrogant doctor who refused to answer her basic questions. Then I called a friend who'd had cancer twice and works in the field. A chain of conversations began. Now, which hospital was the good one, and which was the one where the actor received poor treatment? The conversations went on for a couple weeks between Janet and various friends and family until a reputable doctor was found and the biopsy, which told us she didn't have cancer, was performed. While Janet recovered, I got calls from both her sister and her partner. Both of them told the whole, grueling story of the surgery and hospital experience from their points of view. I wouldn't have sent flowers if Mark hadn't casually said over the phone, what I knew but wasn't thinking about, "Janet loves flowers."

Stories—the small personal ones that bring us close as well as those of the larger world—foster compassion. In the telling of our personal lives, we're reminded of our basic, human qualities—our vulnerabilities and strengths, foolishness and wisdom, who we are. When you hear the details, not just the headlines, about a friend who's lost her job, having once or twice lost a job yourself, you form a bond and, through the exchange of stories, help heal each other's spirits. And isn't this what a spiritual life is about?

Author Thomas Moore writes, "Part of our alchemical work with soul is to extract myth from the hard details of family history and memory on the principle that increase of imagination is always an increase of soul." Only through the expression of our lives can we find their larger, mythic meaning. If they remain unspoken or unwritten, how can we incorporate their meaning into our lives and our cultures, our planet? We need one another to do this.

By telling the larger stories, we extend our vision beyond our own hearths to recognize the enormity of the world and the needs and realities of those far from our own doorsteps. For our caring nature to be engaged, we have to cut through the distance, remove the reasons and the logic that we use to hold our compassion in abeyance, and get right to the place we all ultimately live, the heart.

I'm not, for the most part, talking about news stories, though occasionally they too bring us together. I'm talking about people's first-hand, unrehearsed, sometimes hesitantly spoken events that pass from mouth to ear, from written word to reader. The stories that include not only the facts, but the inner truth, the complicated, embedded details that make world history into people's history, the heart of one person opening into the ear of another. This is spiritual work, to welcome the whole, troubling truth, especially the parts we are afraid to hear, into the living room, the library, our schools. This requires desire, honesty, and a sense of knowing that we're free to express ourselves.

The woman who repairs my printer when it's on the blink calls herself the Laser Lady. When she came by a few months ago, she asked me if my mother was alive. When I told her no, she shared the story of her mother, who had died alone a few weeks earlier because there wasn't enough money to bring her out to California—or to let her daughter go home. It was quite a spiritual moment. Although we each lived in our own memories, those memories came together intimately into the room.

We all live with our losses; they inform us. Yet most of the time those losses are kept in the curtained background. Every now and then we uncover them for each other and come close to the heart of the other. It's not only that others' stories mirror our own experiences, it's that they can broaden what we know and care about.

The spiritual work of writing is a way to keep the gate from locking shut. If there's an avenue to translate your response to a situation—good or bad—you can remain more open, and open is a position from which action can come. Writing is an empowered form of action, which can make it a potent way to respond. John Updike said, "The author is not only himself but his predecessors, and simultaneously he is part of the living tribal fabric, the part that voices what we all know, or should know, and need to hear." It's a dual process, the need to give voice and the need to hear voices—yours, mine, ours.

The Call of Stories

Last summer a report from Kosovo came over the radio on National Public Radio (NPR). It made me think about the impact fear has on us, and what compels us to speak. The reporter said that approximately eighty young, ethnic Albanian women had been kidnapped at the beginning of the war and taken to houses on the outskirts of a village called Cirez. Over the course of the war, neighbors, who had hid in the hills nearby, saw streams of cars filled with Serbian military and police come and go. The villagers believe the women were raped continually. Just before the end of the war, they were all killed and their bodies dumped into three village wells.

About twenty-five feet below the surface, there can be seen three or four blankets of different colors, some red, some checkered, gray, and black. And distinctly under the checkered blanket, there's a shape of a body. You can make out the thigh, the knee, the leg and the foot, and the arm, and it's a shape that distinctly resembles the shape of a human body lying on its side.

I imagine these women alive. I wonder about the details of their lives—what mattered most to them, whom they loved, how they wore their hair, what jobs they held, who their children were. I wonder about the sound of fear in their voices, how the voices of women I know sound when they're afraid. As much as I try, I don't think I have the capacity to truly imagine what it would be like to live for weeks or months in captivity. I've been trying to imagine this for days, but find the thought of enduring such violation every day unbearable.

In order to purchase a transcript of the program so that what I wrote here would be accurate, I telephoned NPR. The operator, Vivian, needed information about the story so she could locate it in the feed for June 30th.

"It's a horror story from Kosovo," I began, and went on with the details I remembered. It was no longer quiet at the other end of the line as I continued telling Vivian what I remembered. She was gasping, sighing, sucking. It did not sound polite. She was crying. I got quiet, listened to the voice of her weeping, and found myself crying with her. "I'm sorry," I said. She kept crying. I listened, and we accompanied each other. Two strangers across state lines, tethered together by sorrow, by the voices of our crying, by the horror of what was so terribly distant from us.

As a writer, I want to respond to what I hear, experience, and am affected by. I never know in advance what will capture my heart and imagination. After hearing the NPR radio report, and then speaking to the operator, I imagined that there were actual sounds left by those silenced voices, and that I carried them. I felt awkward in my body because of a grief that was not mine—but had become mine.

I keep listening for the call of stories because I know my God is there, and though I may not be the "best" writer in the world, just like you, I have something important to say. If stories call to you, you're incredibly lucky. If you're listening, you won't become numb. If you listen beyond your own self, you won't become closed to the world and unresponsive. If you stay open, that openness will bring you to the stories of others, and an authentic response to those stories is what heals us all.

For the Notebook 1

THE LISTENING SELF

As we've discussed, writing is first about listening. This activity is designed to enhance your ability to do just that.

Finding a place where you can be still and (hopefully) uninterrupted will facilitate this exercise and most others. There are times when writing on a crowded bus or in a cafe that's bustling may foster your work, but you won't find it helpful for this exploration.

With notebook and paper in hand begin to attend to what you hear. Give it your awareness. Notice first the most obvious, external sounds. Do you hear a truck's reluctant engine turning over, the early morning newspapers hitting the sidewalk along your road?

Then, coming closer, hear the sounds nearer to you. If you're indoors, what are the sounds of the building—muffled conversations, a clock's tick, the heater's hum, the creaking of wood underneath someone's footstep? Listen also for what the spaces between sounds hold, for the implications of those sounds and what thoughts, feelings, and connections they trigger in you.

Move your capacity to listen even closer. Get a sense of your heartbeat, its sound, the rhythm of your breath, and even the pulse of your blood. What is the song of your body? First, just listen without translating what you hear into written language.

Consider the sounds of your body, the house, and the neighborhood as a sort of daily language. Notice the outer layers of sound. Then move your attention farther inside and then farther out, listening for the voice of your own life's substance and how that is a part of the world's filament of light and dark. You're listening in, as though listening to a conversation in progress, one that's going on behind a few closed doors. You have to be quite still to catch the secret. With this kind of listening, language will begin coming to you. Receive everything: your predictable thinking, your deeper knowing, and what you're not yet conscious of knowing but are becoming acquainted with.

After having listened without writing for ten minutes or so, begin to record what you hear. Note how the act of writing influences what you hear. The paper will hold your words so you can move on to more listening, knowing your thoughts and impressions are being held in place. This is a process of conversing between your deepest self, your larger knowing, and beyond that, your awareness of the world.

What happens if you listen for your pulse, the *I'm here, I'm gone, I'm back* quality? When you listen to your breath, does it change the breath? What does your mind say? What does your heart say? Your spirit? How often have you sat and listened this closely? This is a great way to begin or end a day by giving your attention to the details of the sound-world that surrounds you. And it doesn't take hours either. You can listen closely for any amount of time.

For the Notebook 2

The Voice You Hear

A re there actual voices or metaphoric voices that you listen for? What quality of sound—cadence, lilt, nuance, tempo—do those voices have? Is there a particular person's voice you listen for? When I'm writing, invited or not, I may hear the memory of my mother's critical voice hammering at me, "Don't just sit there; do something!" And, as we'll discuss

in a later chapter, I can never match that voice syllable to syllable. It, occasionally now, towers above me. But I have learned
to respond to it and to allay it by greeting it, holding its fear,
and moving through. My fear of not having enough money
has its voice; it's the sound of a razor-edged saw, cutting back
and forth. There's the caretaker, the benevolent me, who can
coo like a dove, "There you are, honey-girl; write whatever
words you dream to say."

The writing itself has a voice. It may speak in my own voice
or the voice of another; to listen, I have to clear away the clut-
ter in my mind and direct my focus toward what the work has
to say. The voice of the work has a confidence to it that, at
times, I may lack. It knows itself. And the voice may vary,
depending on the work. It may come quickly or ease out like
something expansive emerging from a tight place—butterfly
from enclosed cocoon.

Begin to recognize what you listen for when you write. Is
there a voice? Maybe not. Maybe the words just come silently
and fall lightly onto the page. Whatever you hear, however your
words come, recognize the possibility of messages from within
you and beyond to lead you to writing. Such messages become
a part of a whole, as yet unknown, story.

This activity is one to incorporate into your everyday writing practice, not a stand-alone exercise. So, the next time you
pick up your notebook to write, be aware of what you hear, of
how the words move from your heart and mind to the page.

For the Notebook 3

THE SOUND OF YOUR WORDS

Here are two activities connected to voice and sound.
When you read your work out loud, a connection forms

between breath, heartbeat, sound, and the words. This helps to increase what you know about the material, ensure its veracity, and identify where the piece sings and where it's stuck. By reading your writing aloud, you learn things about it that you won't from reading it silently. It helps you to ask yourself questions about the writing. If there's a missing clue, you'll notice the hole when you read the piece out loud. Have you skirted around something that needs to be told? Are you being repetitive? Where does the language fall flat? Is it true? Take what you learn from reading aloud and work it back into the writing, reading each revision aloud to yourself over and again. I've read nearly this entire book out loud to myself, and it's added to the work significantly. Anytime you've written a draft and you want to come back and develop it, try reading it aloud to see how that affects your process.

Another spoken exercise follows: take a line or two of something you've written, something you like and trust and feel fairly secure in. Read it aloud in your normal speaking voice, with emphasis where it naturally falls. Do this a few times. Try it while standing up or walking around. Then change the volume of your voice and read it in a whisper. Notice how not only does it sound and resonate differently, but the quality of feeling inside you may shift as well. The spirit of the lines is affected by the voice, which may inform the content, giving you new information about the work. This may cause you to revise the lines.

Continue to read the lines in various voice tones. See what it's like to shout the words. Does this affirm them for you? Do you feel embarrassed? Notice how your body is influenced. Your temperature may change. Your cheeks may flush. Notice where in your body the words resonate. Is there a place in your body that distrusts the words? Is it telling you something you need to know? Five minutes of this may be enough at first. But as you do it again, you may find it intoxicating and want to go on for awhile.

CHAPTER 4

JOY IN THE SAYING AND THE POET WITHIN

The girl had a magic bow on her head.
She thought it worked
but it did not work because it was broken.
She still went for a walk though.

Melissa Virostko (age six)

Beware of mirages. Do not run or fly away to get free.
Rather, dig in the narrow place that has been given to you;
you will find God there and everything. God does not
float on your horizon, he sleeps in your substance.
Vanity runs, love digs. If you fly away from yourself,
your prison will run with you and will close in
because of the wind of your flight. . . .

Gustave Thibon

The world of letters is the true world of bliss.

Abraham Abulafia

What if, within you, there was an untarnished, jubilant poet, free of any hindrances? What would she have to say? What might she say to you right now? What are her observations—of the self, the other, the ever-turning Earth? She has her inclinations; they are, perhaps, quirky and often impish. She finds language and the call to language everywhere. She's unfettered. Little daunts her. She sings off-key but she sings; her voice is as big as the moment is inside her.

The other morning, I drove up to my goddaughter's house for a day in the world via stroller. Ella, who is three, greeted me by smiling and hopping up and down on one foot, then the other. Shortly after we went inside, she asked me in her singsong way, as her mom prepared to leave for work, "What will we talk about today?"

What a funny question, I thought. How do I know? "I haven't a clue, Ella Bo, how about you?" That wasn't the answer she was looking for. Still hopping and jumping and happy, but now frowning as well, she repeated her question. Ella wanted specifics.

So I thought back to the last day we'd spent together and said, "Maybe we'll talk about the horse and listen to what he has to say." There's a wooden horse in the children's section of our favorite independent bookstore that Ella likes to ride and who, she tells me, talks.

"What else," she asked, "will we talk about?"

I was thinking on my feet. "Well, maybe we'll talk about the flowers we see growing and how we're making a bouquet for your mom."

Ella smiled. "What else?" she persisted.

"We could talk about the sun warming our faces."

"More!" she said gleefully.

I didn't want to disappoint her. "We could talk about the pigeons who beg for crumbs outside the bakery."

From Ella came another, "What else?"

"Well," I hesitated, "we might talk about the toilet-stroller!"

Now she was in stitches, rolling on the floor, remembering her invention from the day she'd made up a funny story about how her stroller served as a movable toilet.

I kept listing other things, varying the degrees of absurdity, but true to previous conversations, until she didn't ask for more, and by then we were walking downtown and making up new conversations as we went.

The internal, ever-ready poet is always asking questions, always wanting more, wholeheartedly accepting of what comes. She doesn't say, "No, we won't talk about *that.*" There's nothing you could say that would cause the poet within to cringe. She likes odd combinations of words, what some might view as flimsy or irregular. She's curious and faithful. She's put her faith in you and in mystery. Roadblocks are nothing to her; she takes them in a single leap. She takes it all, says, "Why not?" and "OK, what else?" And then, ten sentences later, "What next?" hopping from one foot to the other all the while. She has an infinity of yeses at her disposal. How about you?

It's not like she's never satisfied. She too tires and, sometimes, knows when enough is enough. Then it's time for a nap, and the linoleum floor will do just fine. But it might take her longer to get tired than it does the rest of you—she's a wild child and her hair's uncombed!

CONJURING THE EVER-READY POET

The poet within deserves an invitation. She wants to be called upon. You might create a call to welcome this part of you into the room of your mind and soul. Your writing ritual may be a way to do this. A particular order of initiating your daily practice sets the stage for the creative work. In addition you might create a spell, a series of words to coo the poet within and let her know the coast is clear of obstacles. Or at least the call will alert her to your desire even if there are a few obstructions in the path.

To conjure implies magic. Inclusive forces, those not only of the self but beyond it, have to engage. To summon the poet within involves belief, even reluctant belief, or at least not such overshadowing disbelief that you're likely to ignore what's right in front of you. The poet within represents the part of yourself that has faith in your ability to make something out of nothing. You *can* wrap language around the essence of what you're called to say. The floodgates will open; they're designed that way. When you prepare yourself, the natural and supernatural forces align with that intention. Conjuring is done in earnest with intentionality and faith.

Sometimes in a writing practice what stifles you is a lack of faith. What you're trying to do may seem enormous. If you consider that there's more at work in the process than your individual self, it might free you to delve into mystery and receive language. Take the burden off your shoulders. The poet within knows that stories come from the wind, the trees. She knows that words are sent down to us through the stratosphere. And she'll facilitate their arrival.

Nothing's to say your poet is of the human realm. The poet within may best be described through nature—a wave's curl, the slinking fox. As with the internal critic, discussed in Chapter 5, giving form to the invisible helps concretize it in the mind. It gives you something to hold on to, a metaphor for this part of the self. Conceptualize your poet. Give her (or him or it) form and personality. Once you have its figure clearly in mind, you can place it somewhere inside or outside yourself. At times my poet perches on the shelf above me, fairylike, nodding her head in approval as I write. At other times she's incorporated so completely into who I am that I have no need to externalize or visualize her. Then the writing's like rushing down a river in a smooth-bottomed boat, no leaks anywhere.

THE POET'S TERRAIN

Where does the poet within you thrive, in what environment? What place is freeing to her spirit? And how quickly can you get yourself there—literally or through the imagination? Your poet may need wide-open spaces to run through. Or she may be a walker of late-night streets, like Charles Dickens, who, when he experienced insomnia, walked around London observing the lives of the night people. It may be riding the subway that strikes images into your poet's mind, the clankety-clank speed through the dark tunnels. The neighborhood doughnut stand might appeal to her sweet tooth, that overabundance of sugar, pastry dripping with jelly, and infinite permission

to indulge. Whatever the place, you may find it helpful to your imagination to make a connection between that part of yourself and the
world, to envision the poet within moving in space, as if she were a
physical being, even though she's not.

Can you actually go to that place, where you feel free of limitations
and imaginative controls? If you can break your daily routine occasionally to feed the poet within on a sensory level, you may find your
writing repaid through a lushness of image and a sense of vigor and
freedom to create.

FINDING JOY IN THE SAYING

Joy is at the innermost core of the poet, but it comes from more than
her self. God's in there. The French-Romanian writer, E. M. Cioran
said, "There is a God at the outset, if not at the end, of every joy."
By writing her words, the poet within discovers the unpredictable,
quick-fire delight that comes from creation, from making something
where there was nothing before. In her poem, "The Visible World,"
Jorie Graham says, "Make your temple in the invisible." That's what
the poet within does. She has faith in it and knows that something
unexpected will come out of what cannot be seen.

Consider that at any moment there's so much more going on than
we're conscious of, and this gives the poet within a wealth of image,
experience, and life. Out of that whole bowl, surely something will
present itself to be played with. In her childlikeness, the poet within
lives in the domain of possibility and surprise. The poet Frank
O'Hara is clearly taken by that kind of enthusiasm when he says,
"And here I am, the center of all beauty! Writing these poems! Imagine!" The joy of the poet within is contagious. She has so much, she
wants to give it away, and there you are, lucky recipient. I unbuckle my
hesitation and step out in my Wizard of Oz red, sparkly shoes. The
poet within urges me to put my whole self into language, click my
heels three times, and find myself immersed in a poem.

St. Thomas Aquinas said, "Sheer joy is God's and this demands
companionship." Much joy does call to be companioned. Writing can

help return you to your God within, to the initial joy that's rightfully yours, no matter if it has been forgotten.

There was a story on the radio last week about turtles in Suriname, who, after having not laid eggs for more than twenty years, still know exactly what to do, how and where to dig the hole in the sand in which to lay their eggs. So, even if you've rarely written, that impulse may be just as primary for you as laying eggs is for the Surinamese turtles. It's been yours from the beginning; you're simply returning to that joy when you pick up your pen.

Joy in the Hospital

Joy is not an emotion I tend to associate with hospitals. Though babies are born there and people do recover from illnesses and go home, the overall sense I have when I walk into a hospital is dread and doom. The antiseptic smell makes my heart beat out of sync, causes me to shiver. Hospitals frighten me. My own experience there does not make me enamored of them.

So, when I was invited to Stanford University Hospital by the Art for Healing Program to bring bedside poetry to patients, I wasn't thinking of joy. I packed a briefcase full of favorite poems. They were to be my defense against fear. A list of patients who wanted a visit was prepared. I hoped to read poems out loud and talk about poetry. I hoped that the words might comfort the patients like they comfort me when I hear them read aloud.

I went to Greg's room. I couldn't tell if he was forty, fifty, or sixty. He looked tired and worn out, but he had a twinkle in his eye. His right arm was wrapped and placed in a foam-rubber contraption that kept his arm bent at the elbow and raised straight up. "My first problem," he said, "is this infection in my hand, which is really bad. My second is cancer, and the third is AIDS." He raised his eyes heavenward, tossed his head a little, and sighed. I sighed too and thought, what poems do I have for this life, for this pain? He looked too tired for much of anything. But I know the power of transformation that poetry can offer; even a moment of being lifted to another place might serve Greg. I reached for Tess Gallagher, read her poem "Sudden Journey." "Maybe I'm seven in the open field," the poem begins. In the poem the girl tilts her head up and drinks the rain. Neither Greg nor I could remember exactly the last time we felt that free. "It was a long while ago," he said.

Then I turned to Antonio Machado and read to Greg in Spanish and English. He asked for the Spanish slowly. He asked for poems about love and forgiveness. I read from "I Dreamt." "Sentí tu mano en la mía. . . ." ("I felt your hand in mine. . . ."). Greg asked, "How long can you stay?" "Longer," I replied. While I read, he closed his eyes and smiled. Occasionally, I thought he'd fallen asleep, but his eyes would open just after a poem's last word, and he'd ask for another.

When I asked if he'd like to write, Greg laughed and, grimacing, held up his encased arm. "I could write for you," I offered. "You'd do that?" he asked. I wrote the words he spoke in Spanish, about the man he loves, who's suicidal. He wrote for a long time, having me read his words back to him and then continuing on. He seemed like any writer talking his poem out loud; there was a cadence to his voice, the words coming more quickly as he went, like a jogger finding his stride.

Once we recognize what we feel and voice it, we recognize we can feel deeply and not die from the feeling, no matter how sorrowful it is. The grief Greg felt over his lover's depression and thoughts of suicide wasn't more than he could bear, nor was the sorrow over his own health. When we write what we truly feel, the messy, cumbersome whole of it, a weight lifts and joy begins to enter that space, the joy that's in the saying. Joy has a spirit that brings God closer to us. To speak a truth can free us from holding on to it too tightly. Greg gave some of his sorrow to the words. Joy and relief came in, momentary joy, to take sorrow's place. It was when he got sleepy that I left.

Poems carry our soul in them and allow us to use language in a distinct way that accepts contradictions and complexities, shadow and light. Poems are vessels for the soul. They don't contain it permanently but can hold moments of our quest for exploration and clarity. And they hold our uncertainty with certainty. Gallagher put it this way: "Poems . . . are the best and oldest forms we have for attending and absolving grief, for bringing it into a useful relationship to those things we are about to do toward a future." They help us see who we truly are.

TESTS OF FAITH

When my goddaughter Ella was really little and had just begun to talk, she'd lie back in her mother's arms, the afternoon sun coming in through the picture window, and look out. One day she said, "There's an angel out there." Wendy, who is the kind of mother who will go along with almost anything and has been in the presence of angels herself, believed her daughter. Ella saw the angel many times. She and Wendy talked about it like they talked about everything. By the time Ella turned three, she stopped talking about the angel. Was the age of reason setting down its stakes already?

Your willingness to believe what you cannot see may test your faith in what is true, what is not, and what is likely. At times you have ready faith in the invisible, what's unverifiable, and what's yet to come, and at other times you turn away. Your response isn't consistent. Sometimes you get the goods and other times you don't. The result is not a given. You can sit for hours and hours, and what you write will be dry and lifeless. Or you can sit in that same chair on another day and the words will come with such certainty and surprise, you know you've got to follow and it will be true that the words are taking you to poetry. The unpredictability of art keeps you on the edge.

On the one hand, you have no reason to believe in that next, unwritten thing, which is ultimately a good thing. The edge is an alive place. It makes fuel for the fire. Adventure is not built on reason. Nor is daring. Nor is your attraction to a favorite poem or that painting you're drawn to over and over. But on the other hand, you do have reason to put belief in what may come. The poet within will remind you that you've done this before, and poetry is nearby. It's like there's a small coal inside. If you blow on it, just enough sparks fly and kindling ignites.

Even without reason, would you be stopped, really? Would you curl up into a ball away from your pen because you didn't have reason? If so, give it up now, because art and love and faith require much more than reason. There are many reasons to write. You need them to get you to the page. But reasons are not enough. You need passion and belief to bolster them. You need desire. Desire can overthrow reason. Nobody can give it to you. You've got it already in your cells. That's the reason.

DARING BELIEF

The psychologist James Hillman writes, "The more we hold back from the risk of speaking because of the semantic anxiety that keeps the soul in secret incommunicado, private and personal, the greater grows the credibility gap between what we are and what we say, splitting psyche and logos." The more we hold back from speaking, the farther distanced we become from ourselves and others, the selves within each other. We risk becoming disenchanted and insular, removed, and the more unsure of ourselves we become, the less we feel we have to say.

It's essential to not speak before you're ready. As we'll discuss in Chapter 8, the fallow times may be quiet, but they aren't vacant. But to be burgeoning with your bucketful of ideas, to be reaching for nearby words, or even to feel an undefined impulse to write, and then to not speak is to suppress what you know, which is a form of denial. To turn away from the gift of language is a denial of the sacred self. The poet within retreats, burrows in, sinks down, and is silenced and thwarted. To stray far from belief in your writing is to undermine the work and the self. It's a way of leaving what's essential, your soul, out in the cold while the rest of you comes in. When abandoned, the inner self quavers.

What if you were to believe in the poet within you and in angels at the window and not care that no one else or maybe only one other person, who happens to love you, sees them too? After times of silence, the poet within, wearing her angelic, though tarnished, paper-thin wings will come to your side and dance to a little tune you thought no one knew the steps to. She knows the equation isn't one plus one equals two, which reliably comes out the same each time, but rather the equation is a hummingbird darting above the fuchsia and a ride you once took on a day so hot that the air rushing into the car parched your throat. That equation equals the story you've yet to write.

At the Eye of a Tornado

Sometimes a child can show us the wisdom that pain has to offer, and how we can let images and symbols speak to us.

I met Robert, age eight, in a third-grade class. The children sat around me on the floor and we talked about poetry. Except Robert. He kept himself at a distance, sitting on the periphery of the cluster of children. At first I didn't think anything of it. He was a new boy at school. Another student introduced him to me but didn't seem to know too much about him. Robert didn't look me in the eye when introduced, didn't even look in my direction. I began the lesson, reading a few poems on the theme for the day, that were about where we receive direction and what we follow, who tells us what to do. Robert was lying on the floor behind me, playing with bits of pencil pieces scattered on the carpet. When the rest of the class and I were chatting about ways to begin their poems, Robert was sliding under a group of desks, as though they were a tunnel that might lead him away from the room to someplace else. They didn't. I caught him with my words, said, "Get out from under the desks and join us here on the floor, please." Without a word, he did. The children went off to their desks and began to write. As usual, I walked around the room checking to see who was stuck, who needed a word spelled. Five minutes into our writing time, Robert had nothing on his paper. "I don't like to write," he said. "That's OK," I said, "I don't always either, but we're writing poems now. May I help you?" "No," he answered. I went over to the teacher's desk, interrupted her as she was writing her poem. "What about Robert?" I asked. "Oh, where shall I start?" Her pause was tense and weighted. "It's awfully sad. He's homeless. I think his parents are stoned much of the time. They don't have jobs. Sometimes they remember to pick him up after school, and sometimes it's nearly dark before they get here. He doesn't connect with us. I was hoping you'd have some luck."

I was tired. I'd taught three classes already that day. I didn't want to have to try hard to coax a kid into writing. But what was I to do, leave him with a blank piece of paper and something to say. So back to Robert's desk I went, this time pulling up a chair. There was a picture in pencil on his sheet of binder paper. It was abstract—curved horizontal lines went across the page with some up-and-down scratch marks above them. All of it was lightly drawn. "What's that? You could write a poem about your picture," I said. "Nothing," he said. I got close to him and asked him about the directions that he gets. "Boring, mostly," he said. "But I don't want to write a poem about it." I told him, "You could write about anything." He still hadn't looked me in the eye, hadn't even turned his head in my direction. But he hadn't backed away from me, as kids who want to be left alone often do. His eyes were hooded by a frown. "And if I wrote a poem, I'd probably just trash it." "That would be up to you," I said. "But I think you have things to say. You see, if you write a poem, it's something no one can ever take away from you, even if you lose the poem or you choose to trash it, you've still written it and it will still be yours. You could write your very first poem today." "I might write," he said, "if it wasn't so noisy here." "You mean because I'm talking to you, it's noisy?" "Yeah," he replied. "So, if I go away, you'll write a poem?" "Probably," he said. "OK, I'll go." I got up, and when I came back five minutes or so later there was another drawing. There were circles inside circles, scratched hard onto the paper. It covered the middle of the sheet. Above the picture Robert had written, "I suck." And just below that, "I don't want to write," his truth, solidly there in pencil. "What did you draw?" I asked. "A giant tornado going in circles," he said. "What's it doing?" "It's going to go bye-bye." "That could be your poem, you know." "OK," he said. So I wrote down what he'd said. On either side of the top of the circle were two lightly drawn stars. "What are these?" I asked, pointing to one of the stars. "The stars are shining on the tornado. Now that's it. My poem's done." "OK," I said and wrote the last part down. "Now you've got light shining on your tornado," I said and touched him lightly on the back.

Then it was time for the class to come back together so we could read the day's poems, and I invited students up to the front of the room to stand by the teacher's chair to read. Some chose to have me read; others read their own poems; some declined to share at all. Robert crawled up close behind where I sat and watched the fish in their tank and then stood behind me. Using his teeth, he tied his shirt-sleeves into knots so it looked like he was stuck in a rough version of a straitjacket until the teacher told him to untie himself and put his arms through the sleeves, which he did. When I called his name to read, he said, "OK, but you do it." Robert couldn't stand still. He walked around the room smiling as I read his short poem. The other kids laughed at the "bye-bye" part, so I asked them to be polite and listen carefully and I read it again the whole way through. Robert had come up and stood behind me. When I turned back, he was smiling.

I could have walked out of the classroom with nineteen poems and nothing from Robert because I was tired, but Robert's poem is always the one I wait for, always the one I'm longing to help write down. Now Robert has not only the tornado but an increased awareness of two stars shining down on it, and as we know, even a little light makes the darkness less.

FALLING INTO ERROR

Last night, as I was sleeping,
I dreamt, blessed illusion!
that there was a beehive
within my heart.
And the golden bees
were hard at work

making white combs
and sweet honey
from my old bitterness.

ANTONIO MACHADO, from "Last Night as I Was Sleeping"

I've carried this excerpt from the Spanish poet Machado's longer poem in memory for years, trying to imagine the comb and honey that could be made of my failures. It would be sticky, certainly, in the catacombs of mistakes. In the book-jacket photo, Antonio Machado sits before a well-appointed restaurant table looking dapper in his wide-ribboned hat, tightly knotted tie, one hand over the other, both resting on the top of his cane. There are years and years behind his quizzical, pointed gaze. Those eyes must have witnessed many mistakes, his own and others'. But when I look at that picture, I see the bees in his heart and imagine their buzzing. This is a poem of double error: first, the dream itself is an error, and then, the mistakes of his life. Such enormity to be forgiven.

We can't write failure free. It isn't possible. So give up the idea of perfection. It's the missed stitches and slipped knots that will give your writing the essential *you*. And often it's what readers will lean toward, feeling their own knots undone. If you're looking for a word but can't find it and substitute another, thinking you've messed up, that may be the word that gives the phrase what it needed. And even if you cross it out later, what it's opened up for you in the writing may lead you in a direction you couldn't have gotten to without error. Our humanity and passion lie in error. Everybody makes mistakes. To remove failure from your work would be impossible, and it would remove you from yourself and your potential audience.

The poet within knows I will fail. Still, she pops her gum and rattles off jump-rope rhymes and isn't bothered by failure. But I am. The other day, I failed badly, not on paper but on my bicycle. I was doing my sixteen-mile, get-me-away-from-my-desk-early-afternoon-peddle-fast-because-you-want-lunch-don't-you ride. It was at the beginning of the last set of hills, the hardest part, my favorite part though I curse it, when I downshifted and the chain fell off the chain ring—no traction. Time slowed sharply. I had to peddle quickly to keep from falling and was going nowhere.

Peddling that fast, I couldn't extricate my foot from the you're-one-with-the-bike, sucker, pedal. I had no choice but to fall. Moment of fear, breath caught, then I leaned to the left, fell onto the road and not into the poison oak. I knew the phone company guy who I'd just ridden past parked in his truck eating lunch a few yards away had seen me. Quickly he started his engine, made a U-turn, and left me to my own devices, sprawled in the middle of the road, straddling the bike, and having trouble dislodging my feet from the pedals. A woman in an SUV stopped and questioned me about my status, sweetly willing to drive me home. She wouldn't leave until she was assured that, though shaken and scraped, I was fine. I disengaged my feet and got the chain back on the ring and said to hell with that hill for today, I didn't really like it anyway.

Standing there on the roadside, blood dribbling down my leg, I felt like a complete fool and began to laugh and laugh some more. I had fallen! I'd been on the ground and that was that. I had experienced what I consider a bicycling faux pas. The relief at having made a mistake was distinct. The next morning, the bruise on my arm the size of a mango pit was kind of pretty. The cut on my knee made me feel like I was five again. It was OK.

Sometimes while writing, you're approaching the big hill, you can't wait, you've anticipated this moment for hours, days, or weeks, and then you fall flat on your face. The image doesn't fit the context; what you were certain would work as a closing paragraph has no music in it after all. Whatever the particular failing, you feel it in your body when it happens. The language simply doesn't ring true. It has faltered, as have you. You're afraid people will drive by and see you.

The poet within is faultless and will not blame you; in fact, she thanks you for the show. It's part of her fledgling angelic nature. The poet within won't hold you to your failures; she doesn't define you that way. She wants what comes next and has implicit faith that something will. Words may have defied you, they may have fled, or your voice may be rusty as an old can, yet the poet inside you wants to play. Ever willing, "What else will we talk about?" she asks.

So let your mind go—follow that other train of thought, the one you thought you might be embarrassed or confused by, and see what images you uncover along that route. In other words, don't shun your failures and shrivel up in their presence. They may bring you back to your original idea; they may take you to something better. If you can see your first drafts as exploration, as the domain of the poet within, the freedom will liberate both your current thought and what you might say. Let the language be light to your touch, soft on your tongue.

PATIENCE

Every day I sit here and write. I spend hours in this chair, pretend I've been velcroed here. But I haven't been. I'm here entirely of my own volition. Nothing holds me to the chair but a lust for language and my fear of failure. It continues to delight and amaze me that the words do come. I get up, hang a load of laundry on the line, water the vegetable garden, come back to the chair, a cup of tea in hand. The words return. They were waiting patiently.

What about patience anyway? Is that a place of make-believe in your book? I hope not. To be patient isn't to stop writing or to become passive in the process, but it is to wait, to have space around the words. Often ideas don't come popping out as quick as firecrackers. They have their own time. In writing, time moves in unique ways. You know how it is when you're writing and time disappears. You notice it's nightfall suddenly. But on other days, the time between seconds seems stretched into hours.

At this point in history, expediency is nearly the highest compliment and often ranks above quality. We want the grocery line to be short, don't want to be kept on hold more than a moment. On the road, a car horn honks immediately when a driver thinks the person in front of him isn't going fast enough. *Now* is too far in the past; the future is the moment we're waiting for as we rush to get to another now, some ultimate destination that we never really arrive at but are always impatient to reach. With so many of our needs taken care of immediately, or nearly right away—a pizza delivered at midnight is no problem; stores no longer close on Sundays; in many places, you can buy liquor any day of the week—the idea of waiting is an anathema. If only we had this or that now we'd be fine.

We're always *doing* something. We suffer from a false sense of self-importance: "I need it now!" It isn't the deep selves we're attending to but a continual process of pacification of often trivial desires that takes the place of and covers up the deeper stuff. What are we rushing out of? I think it has to do with feeling and true connection. Where have our souls and spirits gone? Do we think we can buy them back? Not possible. Satisfaction can't always be found in the next thing.

Inside, patient and waiting, the soul sits. Maybe he's knitting a long, long scarf; maybe he's just taking in the view of all this commotion. In Laura Esquivel's novel *Like Water for Chocolate*, when the young woman gets married and leaves home, she gets into the car that will take her to a new life wearing a scarf, and as the couple drive off, the scarf trails behind the car, maybe for miles, the past and the future fashionably connected. Though the poet within is quick in her youthfulness, she is not impatient. She's not getting so far ahead of herself that she leaves herself, you, and a recognition of holiness behind.

If you're writing with patience, you're reminded by the inner poet that the words will come in time. If you're writing without it, what are you writing away from? What might catch you if you slow down and take in the totality of your experience? What if you fall into the open page, blank from top to bottom, and sit there for a few hours? You may not make the traffic light, you may be late for dinner, but the words will fill the paper after awhile. You won't shrivel up waiting. The poet within has plenty of patience to share with you. Just ask for some.

To truly learn anything meaningful takes time. That time may not fit into a predetermined schedule. Writing is a way to connect to the greater longing for peace and understanding, the need for community, the desire for revelation, and the need for meaning. Meaning that gets us beyond our individual cravings and into the depths of soul and spirit, that which binds us to each other, the earth, and mystery. If you choose writing as a spiritual practice, it will teach you that if nothing else. And it will show you how time can unfold you and open the seams of your heart that may have been sewn shut.

Masterpieces

In the days of Michelangelo, when an art student completed his course of study, he produced what was called his masterpiece, the painting or sculpture that he presented to his master to demonstrate what he'd learned during his education. It didn't represent a summation of his life's work. It was his thesis, the symbol of his being ready to launch into the professional world. After acceptance of the masterpiece, the student was recognized as an artist and not until this point would his teacher and other artists let him in on tricks of the trade. Today the term has come to mean the finest work of an entire career, what an artist will be known for.

What if your masterpiece was only your beginning? What might it be? And how much time will you devote to getting to that point? How much will you give to the development of your soul's work? Will you invest in it the way you might your retirement plan or your children's education? Perhaps after years of study you have one poem that truly shines as a thing in and of itself. Could that be enough to carry you into the next phase? And could it simply be a representative statement of all that's gone on up to that point?

I asked my nearly eighty-year-old father what his masterpiece was at the moment. His answer took me aback: "How I lived through the cancer." My father's not one you'd think of as a born-again illness survivor, though he nearly sounded that way. "To have come beside death as I did and then to come out the other side. How's that for a masterpiece?" Just fine, I thought, remembering the treacherous time we'd been through with him when he'd seemed to be a mere breath or two away from dying. His soul had been sandpapered and then been made whole again.

Your writings can serve as markers at various points throughout your practice. In and of themselves they may or may not be what you wish to consider masterpieces, but along with the deepening of your spiritual life, they may be the flags you raise that say, "I was here. I climbed to this peak." Then the work becomes an essential, integrated part of that life.

BECOMING AN AMATEUR

Imagine what you would have said or written at thirty, at twelve, at six. These voices are distinct. How would the writing from ten years ago be like or different from what you're inclined to write now? What qualities are present now that wouldn't have been before?

At twenty what I wrote was frequently lovesick and contrived. The word *gather* appeared too many times; I was trying to hold the pieces together. Personally, it was a desperate time; addicted to cocaine and wanting to write, I was thin and brittle and afraid. The material sounded forced because I'd shut off my essential voice, stridently said "no" to it, and said, "If you're going to be a writer you have to be serious and careful and write within the lines." Not that the books I loved did that.

But to write I thought I had to be someone other than who I was—unseemly, loud, or too quiet, wrong all the way to the confessional. "How many Hail Marys today, Father?" The impulse to write was pure but the writing was not. It gives me the willies to go back and look at my earliest, saved writing. That is not something I often do. I've considered burning it, but empathy for that girl keeps me from doing so. I've had to write my way back to the child's initial inquiring point of view, which is all-inclusive. It's taken years.

The poet within has the perpetual capacity to see things anew. It's a matter of pulling off the layers of being in one groove, of not saying things in the usual way, of being willing to find your own language, your own way into it. This is done through writing, reading, daily observation, and conjuring your poet.

Having worked with children for many years, I see in their writing qualities I want in mine. You can tell they're seeing and writing for the first time—the images and metaphors are new; they connect the unknown to the known in original ways. The sense of permanence and immutability isn't there with children. In general, young children are in the writing for the experience of it. Joy and surprise are alive and fluid. They practice the art of nonattachment without knowing its name. In children who aren't damaged, there's great willingness to try something out, take an idea or a phrase and follow it to see what will come next. We need these qualities in our adult writing, and, as the Irish writer Edna O'Brien puts it, "Writers, however mature and wise and eminent, are children at heart."

At three my goddaughter Ella said, while painting a picture on her big easel, "The moon paints the sky when it's dark." Then there are my students. Seven-year-old Karen wrote, "Future is inside me, right beyond that storm of hope." And when she was eight, Magdalena wrote, "My people are the animals, no matter if they're big or small . . . The little hum of the hummingbird, ahumm . . ." When Frank was eleven he wrote this poem about his grandfather:

My Grandpa's Sadness
When my Grandpa is sad he sings
his favorite songs and plays his guitar.
His heart is on fire. Not just any fire,
a fire like a 50 story building on fire.
He tries to put it out. But he is too sad and weak.

Even in the expression of sorrow there is an embracing, not a closing out of anything. A five-line poem, and we can hear his grandpa singing a sorrow that can be played and cannot be put out. Frank must have known his grandpa well to have written this poem, known him and respected his big sorrow.

Think about the word *amateur*, which is French for "one who loves." If I can write as I love, which is often wholly and is the color red, I can write freely. If I'm willing to see myself as an amateur, I see myself as a beginner. A beginner has permission to experiment, to try, to dare, and to not be perfect. Fine work and even masterpieces can come out of such permission. They're not tied down to such things as accomplishment, perfection, the ideal, failure, and regret. And because they're not tied down, they float free.

The poet within trusts your version, knows that your language will bring you to infinite knowing, that you are directly linked to that knowing, to God, that what you can write is infinite. You may have to dig to uncover the part of yourself that speaks freely and in poetry. So, what are you going to do about it? Are you going to sit and think about writing or are you going to follow the poet's lead? You might get to know this aspect of yourself. You could ask, when your mind clouds over and the forests of your thinking are dark and dense, "What next?" Probably she'll have an answer.

For the Notebook 1

The Poet's Talisman

A *talisman* is an object that is bestowed with magical powers; it can ward off evil. It will protect the bearer. It's helpful to have something tangible to hold on to—a stone to rub, something that fits in the palm of your hand and represents a link to the poet within and divine compassion. What kind of emblem would represent the freedom you're asking for? Think of the weight of this object. It needs to be heavy enough so that you feel its substance. Think of the colors. Is it shrouded or out in the open? Does it have sound? Texture?

On the bulletin board in front of my desk is a photograph of a pastel drawing by my friend, the artist Nanda Current, a mostly underground view of a tree's gnarly, twisted roots. There's only a tiny swipe of area above the ground, just a peek of sky. Nestled below among tree roots is a reddish, ball-like shape. It's tangled there, held. Nothing can untangle it. The bulb sits in the web. It looks sweaty and hot below ground, thick and dense and protected. My internal poet is protected like that; and she's full of more than I will ever see. The bulb in the picture is a seed underground as big as my fist. I think it's indestructible. That's the essence of the poet within me. And though I can't actually hold this bulb in my hand, a warm river rock will do.

Have a lazy afternoon walk through a forest or your neighborhood, keeping your eyes peeled high and low for a representation in the physical world of this invisible, joyful self within. Foraging through one of those overstuffed kitchen drawers, you might glean an object that speaks to you. Put it on your desk to hold in the palm of your hand when you need reminding of the wealth within.

For the Notebook 2

LICENSE TO WRITE

To drive a car, practice medicine, and operate heavy machinery, you need a license. The license verifies that you're authorized to do what you say you want to do. My California driver's license renewal form came in the mail the other day. At the top was written "Congratulations. You may renew your driver's license by mail." Later on in the letter, the Division of Motor Vehicles (DMV) said my new license will be good for five years and that I'd soon receive, once I paid my $15, a new license that would include "the most recent photo from the photo data base." If, in five years, I still look just like that picture, which was taken five years ago, I will be delighted. Maybe what you need to create is the same kind of laminated card to keep in your wallet. You don't even need to pay $15 for this one. Maybe you'd like to attach a little picture of yourself on the corner of it. Then create your own license, find the words that give you the permission you need. Slip it into your wallet and pull it out during those moments when you need to remind yourself that, yes, you are authorized to write. It's called a Poetic License. I got the idea from a poet named Will Stapple who used to give them out when teaching poetry to young people in northern California.

Poetic License
The bearer of this license
is hereby authorized to use words
in order to dive inside and discover the world.
Warning: *Do not enrage the Muse by ignoring*
the privileges granted.
Expiration date: never.

For the Notebook 3

WHAT DOES YOUR POET HAVE TO SAY?

Take fifteen minutes and put them in your room with you. Now, close the door. Open your notebook and pose this question, "Poet, what have you got to say?" See what happens. Just sit back and listen for a few moments and then write down the words that come. It won't take too long. Your inner poet will get the message out to you in the way you're most likely to hear. And down on that paper you'll find the words you most need to cheer you on and urge your voice into uttering the truth.

CHAPTER 5

DOUBT AND THE
INTERNAL CRITIC

We work in the dark—we do what we can—
we give what we have. Our doubt is our passion, and our
passion is our task. The rest is the madness of art.

Henry James

I am listening to several voices, almost all of them telling me
I can't write, give up and watch "Ally McBeal."

Carol Muske-Dukes

Nothing is more desirable than to be released from an
affliction, but nothing is more frightening
than to be divested of a crutch.

James Baldwin

Doubt's a devil of a thing. It can be persistent and rub your knuckles raw, chew your fingernails to the quick. Doubt can cut your words into pieces and burn them right before your eyes. Your room will grow smoky. The sacred self will seem to dwindle, getting tinier and tinier, becoming thimble size, too small to hold even a haiku or one startling, faceted phrase.

There are days when the doubting voice will not quiet no matter how many prayers I say or the number of deep breaths I take. I'm at my desk, my fingers poised on the keyboard, and, just as an idea comes forward, a subtle voice says, "Trash it." So I do. Another thought approaches and the voice, a little louder now, speaks again, the content the same as or stronger than before. Well, after awhile one weakens. Or I do. Then I know doubt's back, and I wipe my brow, take a long, slow breath, and proceed one way or another.

If you put your belief in doubt, it can turn your belief around so that your conviction lies in your weakness rather than in your strengths, your soul, and your curiosity. You've got to be curious about what you're writing to keep at it, and doubt can mess with that. Criticism, whether it's generated from within or from another, can dampen the joyous impulse out of which creativity is born.

What do I wish to believe in—my ability or inability? It was a novel realization when I began to see that I had a choice. One is an invitation, while the other is a rejection. Belief in ability leads to infinite possibilities. Belief in inability leads to nothing good. Belief in ability rekindles your spiritual nature. It implies confidence in what is yet to come, what is unseen and unapparent. If you stake belief in what is beyond you, even in doubt's presence, you can draw from that which is greater than the solitary self to do your work.

You have to choose what to believe and to take valid criticism without letting it injure your nascent writer self. To distinguish between helpful comments that come from within or without and plain nastiness is essential. Is that feedback supporting you and the piece of writing, or is it a slice to the heart? Even after writing for years, there's still the baby writer within whose shell may never get thick and who needs to be remembered. When teaching, I'm careful to respond to a person's writing by commenting on what I see at work in the piece, to make precise comments on content rather than such general comments as, "Oh, that's good." To be simply evaluative doesn't really tell the student much of anything other than the instructor's opinion. As the poet William Stafford said, "We don't revise a piece of writing, we question a life." And our lives are made, in part, of openhearted tenderness that we bring to our writing when we engage our souls and spirits. That tenderness deserves kindness in response. And that openheartedness is part of what makes for fine writing.

Your doubt may not necessarily be about ability, the quality of the work. You may be secure in the work itself but be doubtful of any number of things. What do you doubt about your writing? And does that doubt further the work or stifle it? In response to that inquiry, the poet Philip Levine wrote, "Doubt in the value of writing, the value of life, the value of art, devastates me. . . ." If you doubt the value of what you're doing at every juncture, it's awfully difficult to move forward. It's even hard to stay put. You may spiral downward from one doubting question to another.

The kind of doubt that's problematic isn't the healthy, necessary questioning of the writing. You need that to know if the work does what you want it to do. To ask yourself questions about your material is a way to stengthen it. To know that writing dialogue isn't your strong suit is simply valuable information to have and work with. You need, at times, to be able to stand back from the work and look at it clearly.

Healthy doubt about the work can get you to look deeply at your writing, to ask questions about it that can lead to new directions that support and enhance it. Evaluating and assessing your work are essential, but you have to be prepared for the information. The trick is to take your doubt in stride and keep it in its place, not to take doubt's piece of the truth for the whole kit and caboodle. To take criticism and listen to the doubt without squelching the innate nature of creativity, which is playful, open, and soulful, can, at times, be a balancing act.

Doubt becomes a hindrance when the questioning goes beyond the work itself and becomes an assault on the self. And not only an assault on the self but on God as well, on the essence of creativity, and on the greater forces that are at play behind our writing. When doubting becomes hurtful toward the work, the self, and your faith, it no longer serves you. To doubt your ability or value can temporarily sever the creative, generative force that is yours, where your essential self resides. It cuts off your connection.

The philosopher-historian Rufus Jones reminds us, "Serenity comes not alone by removing the outward causes and occasions of fear, but by the discovery of inward reservoirs to draw upon." Inward fears can be, for some of us, more paralyzing than outward ones, such as community response to our writing, fear of rejection by a publisher, and so forth. In response to any fear in writing, developing inner reservoirs of faith is important; and learning to work with the doubt is part of a writing practice. In this chapter we'll work with ways to respond to doubt and the internal critic, some of which may also be applied to dealing with the outward challenges of a writing life.

THE BEGINNING OF DOUBT

If, during childhood, an aspect of your basic self was repeatedly criticized or distrusted, and you came to believe that you were insufficient or too demanding or a wisecracker, the inner self was wounded. That wound tends to get carried into adulthood and may manifest as self-doubt. If you were told you had limitations when you were growing up ("Johnny can't sing to save his life!"), you may have brought those beliefs about your abilities and your identity with you.

Did your best really not lie in whatever form of expression you tried, or had you yet to truly explore it? If you were told your interpretation of your own experience was incorrect, how can you trust your words now? If you were told you didn't know what you thought you knew, what *do* you know? If you were chastised for your nature, what is your nature now? Deep criticisms of the child-self are forms of denial and abandonment and are deeply injurious. Either you'll accept the veracity of such claims or rebel against them, but in some way you're likely to be affected if you were not seen for who you were and who you might become. Barbs that strike at levels not so close to the primary self are often sloughed off over time. But the negative judgments placed on you about your primary self, at soul level, are many times more difficult to overcome. They cause the soul to contract and withdraw.

When the self is forming, if there is a conflict between the child-self and parents or other important adults, the child tends to embody the conflict. He or she experiences confusion and distress. There's the child's initial way of being or point of view, then an awareness of the parents' response to this, and a third thing, which is the child trying to navigate between the first two, to sort it out, to determine what's true. The child may then disbelieve his initial impulse, may question what he knows, and give it up in favor of the adults' reality. "They're grown-ups. They must be right." The child also may be criticized by someone attempting to be helpful, but this may still cause him to abandon a primary aspect of himself. Doubt may build up like a thick wall.

Some of what is taken from us can become a source of strength. It's like the cut that heals with a large scar. That scar can be a bridge from one side to another if we choose to cross it. The artist uses the wound almost as a starting place, and it opens into places larger than itself. The greater spirit comes through. It celebrates wholeness, embracing what has been lost, making that too a part of the whole self.

Of course, abundant self-doubt isn't a by-product of everyone's childhood. Some people are fortunate to grow up believing in their abilities and inclinations and are free of the weight of doubt's burden. Doubt may not oppress you, but chances are a leveling amount of it comes into your process at times. Or you may get tossed by doubt's wind every now and again no matter how free of criticism your childhood was. The thing about doubt and children is that it doesn't take a cartload to impact the spirit. And you are likely to find that by looking at the doubt and working with it, a freedom in your writing comes to you that you hadn't imagined possible.

FACING THE DOUBT

To engage in a writing practice and to write in a way that honors your complexity as a person and produces material that will reach others requires that you go to your very depths, to the place of questioning, alone. Of course this can be difficult. You may feel the doubt and be uncertain about continuing. Or what you're writing may feel too big for you, but you're compelled to write it anyway. The work may require more of you than you know how to give. You proceed with reluctance, because at times you can't leave that behind. If you know what it is to be doubtful of your writing—to disbelieve its merit and relevance, its clarity, its succinctness, or whatever you question about your work— you probably also know something about getting past that hesitation. If you write your way through, you come to a place of surrender within. The surrender is there in the words themselves. They fill the page and say what you felt called to say. And the feeling changes. Doubt isn't always present. It comes, but it always goes.

THE INTERNAL CRITIC

To have faith in your writer-self and to have faith in God, you need faith in what is unproven and invisible. To have faith in writing is, in a way, to have faith in all that is unformed within you, in all that is unprovable but possible. You give yourself to the mystery and find a knowing sense, faith, and trust that come from within you. You can't rely on an outside force for this faith. In writing, ask yourself, can I stand behind this work? Is my faith here yet? And you get to the place, every now and then, that overrides the doubt. Can you carry the faith you have in God or the earth or the Great Spirit into your own writing? To do so, it will be helpful to see the internal critic for who he, she, or it really is.

You are not your internal critic. The internal critic resides within you. If it weren't for you—your body, your essential self—there'd be no critic. When you feel criticized from within, you may mistake the part for the whole. Not only is it important to not take the internal critic's version of the story for the whole truth, but it's important to recognize this is only one aspect of your mind speaking, not your whole self. The critic may have something valuable to impart to you; he may not.

Duality

If we view the internal critic as one part of the self and the poet within as the other part, we can see that often the critic has the power of "no" and the poet within has all the energy of "yes." The critic may keep us from going so far into the creative process that we are consumed by it and ignore the rest of our lives. The critic serves as a check of reality. "Hey, this might be a good idea, but consider it closely. Support those images; don't leave them dangling there." Meanwhile, the poet delights in the written word and rushes toward the next idea, open armed and openhearted.

In her book *Creation Myths*, Marie-Louise von Franz says, "As long as the opposites are one and in union, no conscious process is possible." There's no friction, no welling up or motivation to get through the portal and write the new story. It can take some degree of dis-ease to motivate us to uncover our truths and write them down. If there's a twofold division, a third thing, the art, can come through that separation, as though along a path between two rows of trees. According to von Franz, every "step toward higher consciousness is preceded by a separation of the opposites. . . . This fact points to the principle that one cannot recognize or realize anything without separating and dividing."

The critic stands at the threshold and cautions the weak at heart from entering into the chaos and rapture of creative work. If you enter this place, you will not come out the same. You will be changed by the spirit of art. The duality of doubt and confidence pushes you toward creativity.

I think of my internal critic as not only the part of me that wants to put the proper punctuation where it belongs and check for logic and congruency, but as the part that's afraid of taking risks, of making mistakes, of being wrong. The critic is the part of the self that doesn't want to appear foolish—anything but that. Meanwhile, the poet within wants to play and take chances and isn't worried about outward appearances at all. Each aspect has its own gifts and the grace of divinity besides.

Holding Yourself Back

At times the critic may simply rag on you. It may sound like this: "You've nothing to say that anyone, I mean *anyone*, will want to read. You've never written anything worth its salt." When the critic makes big, sweeping statements that are more about your character than the piece of writing, you know the internal saboteur is in full force. This self-criticism is hurtful. There's nothing in statements like those that can further you or a piece of writing. They're not meant to. They're meant to repress.

Comments like those come out of fear. What is the critic within you afraid of? Is he afraid you'll spill the beans—tell the family secrets, sell your soul, exceed the limiting confines that were set for you in childhood? Is he afraid you'll do it wrong and embarrass him and your whole self? I find the internal critic to be fearful of experimentation, of moving outside the norm. When you go beyond what's most acceptable, there's greater risk of being told you're wrong. A pattern to follow hasn't been laid out, so the rules and boundaries are less clear. You are more likely to be noticed. The critic doesn't want you to be noticed for fear you'll be made the fool.

The critic is an aspect of the self that's been turned around and assumes the parenting role of control and rule-making to prevent us from being shamed. When we are shamed, we feel hollow inside, and it stings like a million yellow jackets gone out of control on our small self. The critic stops us to prevent a possible failure. But that shutting down closes us off from the self and all the riches that exist there.

Darrie and I have known each other for years. She takes writing workshops with me now and again. I've led poetry classes at the

Homeless Garden Project, a nonprofit organization, where she's a staff member. Recently she sent me this quote by the poet Paul Engle: "Without access to knowledge of self, the writer can make dreams but not art." Beneath it she wrote, "Sometimes when I look at my writing, especially against writing [by others] that I love, it does seem like all I am doing is making dreams and that I almost get to that lucky, exalted state of being, but in the end, turn away and go back, not quite brave enough."

What's Darrie not brave enough for? Where does she feel not brave enough to go? To hold back from that charged place of the words coming on their own is to deprive ourselves of enjoying pleasure and success, of saying what we are called to say, and of contacting the sublime mystery. We hold back out of the critic's fear.

WHOSE WORK IS IT ANYWAY?

Your deep spirit knows that the words must first belong to you. They are yours to have. If, because of early experiences, you've had to question your impulses and have doubted your fundamental self, you may feel drawn to seek the approval of others for your work because a sense of self-trust has been damaged. To look for the acceptance of others prematurely is to leave your own acceptance behind. This puts you at risk of not making clear assessments of your material and of giving the power to do so away. That perpetuates the early injury. If you give the power of approval or disapproval away, you'll always be looking outward, and you may find it difficult to truly receive what comes back to you from others because you have not fed that place yourself first. If you give away the power of responding to and understanding your work, what do you have for yourself?

I encourage you to bring it back. Claim your words as manifestation of spirit and your interpretation of your experiences of the world. Before you look out, look in to the material and ask *yourself* what you would be inclined to ask another. Find your own answers.

RESPONDING TO THE CRITIC

I've worked with many adults who at some point in their education were told, "You can't write." The earlier it's heard the more potent it is, and that message goes under the skin and can stay there like some prickly allergy that surfaces as an itchy rash whenever you put pen to paper. Writing is not just a tool we use in a daily, practical kind of way—grocery lists, reports at work, letters, and so forth. It's also a way to give voice to the soul. The next few sections provide suggestions for you on how to keep your voice even when the internal critic comes calling.

Meeting Your Critic

I've found it helpful in my own writing and in my work with students to personify the internal critic so it can be seen as one aspect of the self, just like the poet within. My critic is tall, rail thin, like I'll never be but just as my mother used to be. She dresses in Armani. Her stockings, yes stockings, never run. She wears six-inch, black patent leather stiletto heels, which are against my politics. And she drives a yellow, gas-guzzling Corvette, equally against my politics. There's such a cleanliness about her, cleaner than Ivory soap, that on first glance you'd think she was never anything but kind. But she appears at times when I'm writing and tells me I'd be better off cleaning something. She is a parody of my mother, but in the moment she appears I can't usually see that.

Sally, a finance officer who took a workshop with me a few years ago, described her internal critic as a large man, about fifty years old, who lives inside her. He resembles no one she knows personally. His bulky jeans slip below the elastic of his underwear when he walks. When he enters her room, his girth stifles her small frame. At times when she sits to write he smothers her words, smoking a dainty panatela all the while. His voice is big and booming and says, "Honey, got a light? Give up that story, why don't you? Your words are made of putty, they're pasty and thick. You've gone dry, dry's all you've got. Give it up. It's just an empty wish anyway. . . ."

Through working with imaginary figures, we can disarm our critics to some degree. Sally feels kind of sorry for the big man who intimidates her. I loved my mother, but I don't love her in the solely critic form. That love has helped me to soften and sometimes disarm my critic. Banishment didn't work, though I tried for years. It's empathy for that part of myself that has made the greatest difference. It has taken a long time to get to this point, but I try to have space for my critical nature.

Working with the Critic

The poet Naomi Shihab Nye told me the following story:

> I was lucky in my twenties to hear [poet] Edward Field give a talk here in San Antonio. A student asked him about doubt, if he ever suffered it. And the answer he gave has been like this torch in my mind ever since. He said, "Of course I have doubt. I invite her over for dinner and then I send her on her way. I've befriended her. If I'm an artist living an artist's life, doing these things, then of course I will be visited by doubt. If not, there would be something wrong. She's my recurring house guest."
>
> [She's] the passing guest of doubt. If I treat her well while she's here, maybe she won't stay too long. So, now, when I have doubt, and of course I do, I think, OK, what do you want to show me this time? What shall we talk about? I've been able to personify it more since he described it in that way. I don't let it become this huge, gripping, paralyzing force. I know, just like when I'm in a grumpy mood, one of the gifts of maturity, I'll just get through this.

What might the critic have to show you today? It could be helpful information: the story's plot has fallen into a dark hole, or the poem's lost its rhythm. You could need what the doubt has to show you. So you might want to try Nye's technique of asking the critic what she knows. Maybe that will help you have a comfortable relationship with it. If the information's valid, you can take it and strengthen your work that way.

It's helpful if you can stand back a bit and watch the critic in action and listen to what he's telling you. Witness your response to the criticism. Actually stop writing, face the voice, and listen. Free yourself of the encumbrances of self-doubt, and ask the critic, "Now, what were you saying?" Listen to the answer. Notice if it's substantive, "The third line from the bottom is flat." Or "This doesn't make any sense. I don't understand it." There may be information that's helpful to what you're writing. The critic may have something to say that will advance the work. These comments are direct and constructive. They apply to specific things in the writing.

Turning to Face the Bully

My student Laurie remembered and wrote the following story in one of our workshops. It's not actually about the internal critic, but it makes a point that might support your process. You might find that turning to face your critic like it's a mythological monster makes it shrink as a result of your calling its bluff.

It was a long walk to the store from where I lived. We lived at the farthest end of the street—the apartments ran from one end to the other, out to the Parkway, across the ditch that ran down the middle of the Parkway. Almost at the end of the street, somehow I heard him behind me. A boy, from the street one over, a few years older than me and about a foot taller. We didn't know each other but I'd seen him over the years. Somehow the street one over seemed like a different country—my world was the apartment complex and all my friends lived there.

Without saying anything he started throwing the small, hard, unripe olives from the trees that lined the street at me. It was so out of the blue, so unprovoked. The first millisecond of reaction, fear; the next anger. I ran directly toward him, an olive's throw from me. He suddenly turned and began to run away, but embarrassed to run from a girl and especially a girl so much smaller than himself he turned back and rigidly withstood his fear, planting himself where he stood, trying to adopt an attitude of fearlessness and intimidation, pulling himself up to his full height.

I came up to him, stood directly in front of him, and slapped him across the face as hard as I could. We both stood there, me looking at him intently, he looking back, taking in my lack of fear, my small size, my intensity, my unwillingness to be intimidated. There was no opening. He stood his ground, but he was the frightened one and we both knew it. He slowly turned around and walked away.

Hold That Doubt

In the face of your power and certainty, the critic may crumble. He may turn and go and leave you to your work. If you feel a softer technique is called for you might try mothering this part of yourself.

My friend Wendy suggested this to me once, and I've returned to it often when doubt gets wedged in tight between me and what I have to say. Imagine your internal critic could fit in your arms, like a baby. If you rock the critic and sing to it like you would a frightened infant, it will soften just like the bully. A walk around the block is a good idea. I'll get in the car and drive to Point Lobos, famous for its ocean view and personally famous for being a repository for my doubt. I walk that doubt around a loop that takes me to the cove at China Beach as if I were walking a sick baby. "There, there, darling; it's OK. Sure, you want to rage a little more, go on; I'll hold you," I say, whispering so the other walkers and picnickers won't hear. It's the way in which that critic-self is met and seen and received in his fearfulness and, through being met, is calmed. Think of the martial artists who walk directly toward their opponents and employ the opponents' energy to disarm them. An ease comes through, doing this, and then you can carry on with your work, attending every now and then to that frightened self, small and needful of care and attention.

The Benefits of Rest and Reprieve

Some days I need to get up from the chair, brush off the seat of my pants, go down to the basement, and howl back at the doubting voice. Then, I take a blanket outside into the sun and rest, collecting rays like a bee collects pollen. Later, I can take the criticism and maybe make something from the sourness turned sweet. And some days nothing should be made. There are times when sitting at the table for hours does no good and a break is needed. Contrary to my persistent nature, rest is often what's called for when I'm being self-critical. A day off may do more to recharge my creativity and my confidence in it than continuing onward like a good puritanical writer. Having been raised with the ethic of "Work harder and longer, work better," it's not my nature to accept that harder and longer don't always mean the result will be better. Sometimes my critic appears when I have been working hard and long. It may be the only way I can convince myself to take a break. And a little distance helps me to see what's really there in the writing and what isn't. A sense of balance and perspective can return when I'm not running on empty.

Not only is rest helpful to the creative process when you feel doubtful, but at other times, a rest can add to your stockpile of words more than being at your desk for hours. Writing isn't like building a fence, so your arms won't tire, but your mind and heart will. I suggest you give yourself breaks and don't wait for the critic to hammer you into doing so.

Try doing something physically challenging. A writer friend of mine goes to the gym and does twenty-five-pound arm curls. She sits on the padded bench in a windowless room and does ten curls with each arm and then again. She may do a third set, if she's got it in her. She grunts a little. By that time her biceps are pumped up, firm and shiny with sweat. She gets up, stretches, goes home, and after a shower, she's ready for words again. And they're eager for her.

The writer Irving Stone knew the value of changing activity, the view, and the climate. He'd put his hands in the dirt. "When I have trouble writing," he said, "I step outside my studio and into the garden and pull weeds until my mind clears—I find weeding to be the best therapy there is for writer's block." It's true for me too. There's something about putting my bare hands into the soil, scooping it up, digging down, that brings my mind back home. It literally "grounds" me and allows me to breathe free of the constraints of doubt. There are weeds to pull at instead of at myself.

Usually though, I take to my bicycle and ride into the hills. After a few miles of climbing, the hills begin to do their magic. To climb I have to enter them. To enter them is like entering language, blindly going forward into what may come next, trusting the body, the soul, and the mind. A place of faith. Entering them I begin to write. Not exactly what I was planning to write but something that would sit next to it. The words start coming like delicate waves reaching the shore and sinking into the sand.

Any of these responses to the critic or ones that you make up yourself can serve you. What's most essential is to recognize when the doubt has value, when it does not, and to respond to it so that your creative self may deepen and shine.

For the Notebook 1

JUST WHO ARE YOU, ANYWAY?

You might personify the critical voice, give it an actual form, name, voice, stature, even imagine the car he or she drives. This externalizes and concretizes something that's a part of the mind. If you can visualize the critic as its own entity, separate from yourself, it's easier to work with. You can make distinctions between the poet within and the internal critic and see how various aspects of your mind function. Grab some art materials, whatever you've got around the house: crayons, markers, and some large paper. You don't need anything fancy. Close your eyes for a few moments, and let yourself feel the presence of the critic. Does it have a human or nonhuman form? Is it large or small? Female, male, or genderless? How's it dressed? Does it smell good? Is it hairy? You might want to give this aspect of yourself a history, name, and residence all of its own.

When you're ready, begin to draw as you feel inclined to, allowing the drawing process itself to also tell you the shapes and colors of this critical self. When you feel finished with your drawing, stand back from it and see who you've created.

Through having created this piece, when the critic comes over you, you have an image and a fairly total sense of who this is, which will help greatly in working with it. Instead of a nebulous sense, you'll have a picture. It helps the process when we can see who we're dealing with. That bit of clarity, like a magnet, draws more clarity to it. Next time you're burdened by self-doubt, you may want to ask the critic to wait and take a nap and come back later for the editing process. You may want to give it a chair.

If you set aside an hour or two for making the critic out of paper and for writing its words, you'll have plenty of time. Plan on at least fifteen minutes for writing and expect a page or two of words. This activity also works well for creating a vision of the poet within. The paper poet who's on the wall in front of my desk has a blue face, body, and dress. She wears a red cape emblazoned "Super Poet," and on the front of her dress is a strike of lightning. She also, of course, wears a construction-paper crown.

For the Notebook 2

The Words Themselves

During a time when the critic's loud, take out a clean sheet of paper and write exactly what you're hearing, word for painful word. You'll find that as you write, more words come to the surface. Write whatever you hear that stymies you, no matter how it sounds. You're not going to show this to anyone (unless you decide otherwise). You may find this takes awhile—a half hour, an hour. It's OK. This counts as writing time. And if you don't stop and listen, the litany will likely continue, anyway, which means you'll be hearing it and you'll be burdened by it—in which case you'll feel like horse dung by the end of your writing time.

After you write down all that you've heard, try responding to some of it. Rewrite a sentence at the top of a page, and, with as much of your kindness toward yourself present as possible, respond. Tears may come, so grab a Kleenex or two. Pay attention to your responses and how your body feels. When I do this I notice a lightness come over me, kind of a floaty feeling, like after a half glass of wine, only better, with no fuzziness to accompany the float.

For the Notebook 3

Back at Ya

When the critic's not harping on you and you're not feeling the pressure of self-doubt, you might think about the times when you do and the ways you can respond the next time. Say you're hearing the critic's voice in your ear, quietly first, then louder. What can you say back? We've talked about holding the fear and other possibilities; but what words do you want to have in your storehouse of responses? What do you most need to hear when you're being self-critical? Or what is it you'd like to see? Can you visualize it? Sometimes when I can't sleep at night, I imagine a still lake and myself out there in a tidy little boat, just floating around, nowhere to go, no hurry to get there. When I hear my critic, I'm running for that boat! What I want is someone to protect me, and I've got to be the one I call. If you can put aside a couple of responses and have them ready, then when the time comes, as it will sooner or later, you'll have something to help you move through the hard part.

For the Notebook 4

A Conversation Between the Internal Critic and the Poet Within

The internal critic is brother to the poet within. Are they estranged? Why have they turned away from each other? Do they look at each other, growl, and show their teeth? Are they in complete opposition? Or are they slightly distanced members of the same family? How you see their relationship will influence the quality of your writing life.

The writer's self is in the center. On one side is the poet within, and on the other is the internal critic, your two angels. Is the critic your Lucifer, the fallen angel who was once God's favorite? The writer self mitigates and at times arbitrates between them, that is, when the self is strong enough to do so. I never worry about being consumed or overthrown by my benevolent poet, no need to. But I have to watch and decide when to take for doctrine the "advice" of the internal critic, who speaks with such authority.

Invite the two to take a seat and have a conversation. Get out your notebook and write down what you hear one and then the other say. You might referee this conversation for a half hour or so and end up with a couple of pages of dialogue. Be sure to reread what you've written before you close your book. You might give yourself a few minutes to write down your response to what you've just read.

CHAPTER 6

BEGINNING A SPIRITUAL WRITING PRACTICE

Whatever you can do or dream you can, begin it; boldness
has genius, power and magic in it.

Johann Wolfgang von Goethe

In the beginner's mind there are many possibilities; in the
expert's mind there are few . . . that is the secret of the arts:
always be a beginner.

Shunryu Suzuki

I write unimportant poems because I am human and gross
and have nothing to say. I am, however, a language
supplicant. The language is wiser, deeper, more sentient,
and more haunted than anyone who uses it. I mean only to
woo the language, to submit myself to it as best I can, and
to hope that when I have harkened to it humbly and
gratefully, it will now and then empower me. . . .

John Ciardi

To prepare yourself to receive language, you put yourself at the threshold of the soul and give your work a quality of attention akin to prayer. At the forefront is the call to manifest imagination and spirit into words. It's a kind of asking; you're reaching toward what's almost beyond your grasp. You long for the words on the paper. Writing makes longing evident. It's what gets the writer to the well, to the shared source of creativity.

To have a writing practice means you're actively engaged in something that isn't finished. It's a process. By committing to writing, you elevate it and confirm its value in your life, revere it as a sacred act. This sanctifies an ongoing endeavor. The only way to get good at most things is to practice doing them. Yet the practice is never the same. Day by day it changes. Some days you'll feel expansive, others contracted. Some days you'll get far, and on others you won't even get to the end of the page. A writing practice has its dips and dives. But how do you engage in an ongoing process of soul-speaking that will give you a vessel to contain your written possibility?

The French writer André Gide said, "I never produced anything good except by a long succession of slight efforts. No one had meditated or better understood than I Buffon's remark about patience, 'Genius is but a greater aptitude for patience.' I bring it not only to my work but also to the silent waiting that precedes good work." An acceptance of your "succession of slight efforts" and a patience to bear them are essential to practicing the art of writing to enhance the life of the soul. The idea of perfection is only illusion anyway. The best effort comes through the day-in, day-out practice of putting the pen to the page.

FUEL FOR THE FIRE

When I asked a number of writers, "What fuels your writing?" I received various responses, but what linked them was a clear sense of need and desire to create. Poet Philip Levine answered, "I began believing poetry, even mine, could make the world and those in it

better. But some years later—at age twenty-five or twenty-six—I realized that if no one is reading poetry it can't change a lot, though what
I had read changed me enormously. By this time I had fallen in love
with poetry and the process of making it, and I just kept at it out of
that need." Perhaps Levine's poems do make a difference; they've made
a difference in my life, showed me new ways of seeing, introduced me
to people I'd never have met otherwise. Maybe we're not meant to
know the influence our writing has on others—at least in the short
run. Reading changes us; it affects how we view the world, and then
our actions are influenced by that. A chain of events may follow from
those words that we read and love.

Poet Joy Harjo describes her need: "I perceive my impulse to write
as a human need to emulate the Creator. We are active creative forces
. . . and can't help but create as we move through our lives." After all,
life is creation. The writer celebrates life's various forms in an attempt
to find and make meaning. The poet Naomi Shihab Nye finds that
life exists not only in the grand but in the infinitesimal. "Where's the
meaningful pulse, where's beauty? Where's something tiny and noble
that could gird this day?"

What's the fuel for your writing? If we, as Harjo, can see our need
to write as being as natural as God's creation, then what could hold
us back from the page? How could we deny a need that primary and
essential? Does your call to write wake you from sleep or refuse to let
you sleep? Does it come over you in the middle of conversation or
when reading a good book? Is there a hidden desire you're driven to
make manifest? If you begin a writing practice you'll find that the
fuel gathers and the fire grows.

CYCLES IN WRITING PRACTICE

Fluidity is a primary part of a writing practice; staying open to what
comes. It's a circle but it also walks a line—beginning, middle, end.
Every piece of writing has those three components. When we're writing, we're always moving toward one of them. And yet, we also have

to be in the immediate moment of this sentence, this word, and not jump ahead to completion. According to Anne Baring and Jules Cashford, authors of *The Myth of the Goddess: Evolution of an Image*, during the Bronze Age, "The individual phases [of the moon] could not be named, nor the relations between them expressed, without assuming the presence of the whole cycle. The whole was invisible, an enduring and unchanging circle, yet it contained the visible phases. Symbolically, it was as if the visible 'came from' and 'returned to' the invisible—like being born and dying, and being born again." There within each piece of your writing, is the whole; it exists, invisibly, even before you get there.

At times you may actually write the ending of the piece with only a glimmer of the rest and then you'll go back and write to that end. Or you may know both the beginning and the end, but the middle will be unclear. Sometimes a piece will be built around a particular character or upon a sound. Often the ending is not known when you begin, and you write toward something you don't know, uncovering clues along the way to direct you further.

In writing practice we can be overly attached to production, to bringing material into the light, and we may feel a tremendous sense of failure during the fallow times. Be attentive to the fact that the writing process is, like the phases of the moon, a cycle. The more you write, the more you'll experience this as true. Not easy, but true.

A primary way that I verify my inner life and its value is by writing. If I'm not writing, I tend to feel invisible, kind of gray, not whole. But the cycles of the writing process include periods of not writing. Then I have to hang out in that place for awhile, just be there with all the accompanying discomforting feelings. Our culture these days is so bent on productivity, immediacy, gratification, and results. Children line up in advance for the newest Harry Potter book. Many reserve their copy weeks ahead of time. Part of me thinks, great, reading's gaining in popularity; less TV, more books. But what this frenzy reeks of more than a reading craze is an I-gotta-have-it mania. The desire for satisfaction and immediate gratification is intense. Inclusive in a spiritual writing process are periods of not having, of being without, of longing. If you negate a part of the process, you may end up with product, but that product may lack soul.

Part of being in the process is staying in the present with what you write. To seriously consider what you might do with what you've written before you've written it—a reading down at the cafe next week, submission to that new literary magazine you just saw—is like putting the cart before the pony but still expecting him to pull. You have to write the piece to unveil its identity, its form, and second to discover its life, where it will go, where it will take you.

BEGINNING TO PRACTICE

Imagine yourself as a fishing pole and line. Perhaps a fish will choose your hook. The other day, at a beach near Big Sur, I saw two fishermen at the water's edge. The handles of their fishing poles were buried securely in the sand so that the poles extended high up into the air, and then tipped forward, the lines reaching down into the water's depths. The lines bridged known to unknown, shallow to deep, light to dark, air to water. I imagined the bait wiggling in the sea and the hungry fish eyeing it, trying to decide if their lives might be worth this one bite.

That's how it can feel at the initial stages of writing. Could this word be worth everything if I were to write it down? When we stand on the edge between words and no words, that's what it's like. In "The Journey," the poet Mary Oliver asks, "What will you do with your one, precious life?" When it comes to writing, the risk is "Can I do it; can I say something meaningful?" Given that many of us live— every now and then, anyway—in the fear of not being or having enough when it comes to creativity, it isn't surprising there's a reluctance to risk cutting our tongues on the fish hook for the sake of food for the soul.

Initiation implies risk. It requires belief. The first step to committing to something is to begin it. That something is bigger than you are. When you begin something, forces outside yourself align and support your endeavor. Writers give themselves to the practice. This is a form of love. That giving prepares writers to receive the magic of creation, moving writing beyond the mundane and into the celestial. Plato said it this way: "First a shudder runs through you, and then the old awe creeps over you." There may be hesitation and fear, but then the writing takes over. Every day I feel gratitude for that awe, for initiating a process whereby I will say more than I ever thought I could.

Before a writer commits himself, he remains on the outside. He can only stand at the gates and look in. To make writing yours, you'll need to enter it just as you would a house. You'll get to know writing as a spiritual practice by practicing it. Writing spiritually is a way of making, and then keeping, a promise to yourself, to God, to what may come and where language may take you. Carl Jung said, "I permitted the spirit that moved me to speak out." To begin a spiritual writing practice, the writer invites and allows the spirit to speak.

Sit down and see what you're drawn to say. It may not be the idea you think you know the most about. Often we write to find out what we know, to discover the mysterious connections between this and that. The poet Lucille Clifton tells us, "I do think that poetry is about questions. . . . I don't write out of what I know; I write out of what I wonder. I think most artists create art in order to explore, not to give the answers. Poetry and art are not about answers to me; they are about questions."

It's sort of like you're playing tag and the kid with the striped shirt just touched your back. Now you're "it." You're the writer making stories. Even if it's for only an hour or two or for every morning of the rest of your life, what you'll get from writing will depend on the attention and devotion you give. The poet Jane Kenyon described this kind of awareness: "You really have to turn your complete attention to something large, something that makes you forget who and where you are and what you have and what you don't have. You have to bring your awareness completely to this new thing." This is true about the practice of writing as well as whatever you're writing about.

In the midst of writing, the activity itself stands at the center of your life; it's the focus. Everything else slips to the background. You are in the service of the story. All of who you are goes into its making. The story travels out of you and becomes its own thing, separate from you. It requires your love and devotion to become itself. The fact that it's your story no longer matters. Whatever you're writing, you might try saying, as though speaking to a person, "Tell me about yourself," and wait for the answer. Even if you're writing about a jar of buttons on your shelf, that jar and the connections you make with it become the center of the universe for the moment. So much of the practice is about waiting for the story to unfold, and being there on a regular basis so that it and all your stories have a place to be received.

To begin writing is really quite simple. You need paper and pen or pencil, time to write, and a place. To make a practice means that writing isn't happenstance; just like with other things that are important in your life, you make time to do it, and then you show up and write. Take your notebook off the shelf and write anything! See what you can turn a shopping list into. You may want to begin with some of the writing exercises and suggestions in this book, or perhaps there's already something calling to be said, and all that's been missing till now are the components of practice, ritual, and promise.

Determining What to Write

I'm not always sure who determines what I write. Is it great energy pressing into me, the Muse, my past, the political environment, the natural world, the life of my dreams, or the lives of my friends? All of it. At any particular time, when I'm about to begin something new, I get that feeling like I'm sitting before a lined-up row of dominoes. I push one and, rat-a-tat-tat, they all fall down. Writing's like being on a fast train. I look out and see every scene and the phrase that's up next, ready to be written about.

When I decided to write this book, I didn't really decide. It's as though the book chose me. There are other books I want to write, another I've begun, but this one kept raising its hand, saying, "Pick me! Pick me!" I'd have been coldhearted not to. One of the most important things about beginning a spiritual writing practice, as we discussed earlier, is trusting the words and where they'll lead you.

One of the advantages to having a subject is that when you sit down to write you have a starting point and don't need to generate one in addition to the words themselves. You may find it helpful to your process at times to give yourself topics and stick to them. And yet there's nothing like stumbling onto a subject through writing one word after the next until—there it is, the thing you most needed to say.

There will be times you'll have your subject in your zip-up pocket and other times it will unscroll itself to you as you walk from one stepping stone to the next. Both are adventures. Both will take you where you have never been before.

KINDS OF APPROACH

My work is driven by either content (derived from feelings, thoughts, and the desire to pursue a specific idea through writing) or impulse. The former may be outlined in advance. It may have sections and categories, and it will be clear from the beginning that a particular progression of thought will work whereas another won't. Even within highly structured writing, there's room and need for adventure of thought and spontaneity. The difference with a piece of writing whose subject is predecided is that even if I go off wildly into surprising directions, it's got to hold together and form a logical and cogent whole.

If I'm writing in my notebook with no end in mind, just out for a stroll or run through language, there's nothing more required of me than to write and write, unhampered and free. That writing comes out of an unspecified, driving impulse to speak. I may also need to say something particular that will never be for anyone else's eye. The focus of the For the Notebook sections that conclude each chapter is primarily to support writing for spiritual exploration, to give you a way to focus your writing and expand it. You may find that some of what you're writing you want to develop and revise for hours, for possible publication or for sharing with friends.

You may not know just what your notebook holds till you go back later and reread what you've written. There will be some days when you sit down to write that you'll have a fairly clear sense of where you're going, which wilderness of words you're entering—one with no path where you have to travel cross-country or the other with the wide, dirt trail. You'll be motivated by having something particular to write about and, though the exact words may not be known, you'll have an initial way into the material. In addition to having a direction for the content, its form may be apparent from the get-go ("Oh, it's a poem I'm writing.").

The approaches are not the same. How I look for words is influenced by what I'm looking for. When I'm working on an essay, something directed from outside of me, I've got a destination. When I'm writing a poem, the experience is distinct from other writing. There are few road signs and none that really give me any indication of where I'll end up.

Author Maxine Hong Kingston talks about her ways of approaching writing:

> *I have two methods of working.* One of them involves tapping the sources of creativity, that part of the self that for me includes a higher vision of what is going on in life. I don't have a controlled way of going about that. I might be anywhere when it comes, and I could end up writing all over the floor or up the walls and not know what's going on. It's like having a fit. . . .
>
> The second method is following a trail made by the words themselves—by sitting down and writing, writing crazy, writing anything, fast. The words include the vision. That rush, that outpouring—that vision or high or whatever it is—doesn't last very long. A lot of writing gets done in a very short time, but it's not

very good writing. Often it turns out to be just a reminder about how something felt. It has to be reworked. Most of my time goes into that rewriting, which I have much more control over. I come back to the original material, think about it rationally, rewrite it and reshape it.

WHEN ENOUGH IS ENOUGH

How do you know when you're done? When is enough enough? I've been in a number of elementary school classrooms teaching poetry and said to the children, "We'll write for about fifteen minutes." After a mere five minutes, a hand goes up. I walk over to the child. He says, "I'm done." I think, and have unfortunately said more than once, "How can you be done, you've only been writing for a few minutes?" I'm thinking at that moment not about this kid but about what writing's like for me. I think I could spend an entire week on one paragraph, writing and rewriting it dozens upon dozens of ways. But if I look down at Billy's paper and read what's there, I find he's right. The poem is done. Which is to say, you can't determine when a piece of writing's finished by how long you've been working with it. It's done when it's done. Enough is enough only when it is. And you know by how your mind-soul-body feels. It's like the last domino in the row of dominoes has dropped. You may have touched the first one an hour ago, but depending on the length of your domino row, it may take that long before the last one's lightly pushed down by the one before it.

This may not be the final ending of the piece. If you move into revision with it, the whole thing—not only the ending—may change. But in a given writing session, if you pay attention and tune your focus in to your work, chances are you'll have a sense of integrity about the ending you've come to. And you'll know that later you may revise. It comes back again and again to trusting your self. And we get there through faith and experience.

To Revise or Not to Revise

The idea that a first draft is a finished draft is, in general, pure illusion. I've heard that poet Mary Oliver spends fifty hours revising and has, by the completed poem, seventy drafts before she gets to the final one. What I look for in a completed poem of my own is to be able to say yes not only to every word in it, but to the relationship between each and every word. William Stafford puts it this way: "A poem is like a spider's web; if one part is touched, the whole would tremble."

The methods of revision I find most useful are different for poetry and prose. When it comes to poems, they always begin longhand. I've never kept a poem I've begun at the typewriter or computer. There's something physical, visceral about writing poems, and for that I need to hold a pen between my fingers and feel the smoothness of paper under my hand. I want the notebook on my lap. I want the feel of my thighs against my belly and to lean over my knees sometimes. The first few drafts are handwritten. The actual word changes are made through writing the poem over again and feeling either "Yes, that's right" or "No, not that word." And I don't catch everything that needs changing in a first rewrite. On average, I think I rewrite a poem five to ten times by hand. Then I move to the computer and continue the process. The nice thing about working at a computer is you can see the piece in front of you, clean and clear with lots of white space around it. It's there I really begin the work of line breaks in earnest. I can try the breaks four or five different ways, print them all out and see what works. As we discussed in Chapter 3, reading out loud can be extremely helpful in revision. With poetry, reading the poem aloud helps me determine where one line should end and the next begin.

With prose I begin either by hand in my notebook or at the computer. I find the speed with which I can type helps my prose work. I can write nearly as fast as my mind's buzzing along. And I like seeing my words neatly before me instead of scrawled in my notebook. The luxury granted by computer to cut and paste, to rearrange words and paragraphs, to move whole pages, not only expedites the process but mimics the way I change my mind and then change it back. Sitting on the floor of my study with slips of paper all around me, I sometimes choose to literally cut and paste paragraphs by hand. For me prose doesn't require the body contact with the words themselves that poetry does.

There are times when what's essential is to write free from the thought of revision. To write deeply, from the essential, spiritual self, you need freedom. To get free, it's important to feel unharnessed by the constriction of revision. Write what you're going to write, read it over, and then put it away, close the book. Maybe another day, say next week, if that piece of writing calls to you, look back at it and see if you want to build it into more than a notebook entry that was written just for the experience of the telling. If you write with a finished product in mind all the time, you may tie your hands and keep out your most outrageous and dangerous thoughts, your best writing.

A SEPARATE NOTEBOOK

At times you'll lose a thought like a frog jumping away from you. You'll be madly writing and think that the next thing you're going to say is in line just behind what you're saying, but when you get there it's gone. A dreadful feeling. But most of the time thoughts call again; they come back. It just may be awhile. So proceed to what seems to be coming next and follow that rather than fixating on what's gone. When the thought or impulse does return you may find it enriched, heightening and in possession of more of itself.

To hang on to slippery thoughts, you might try jotting a note down in the margin of your notebook. When I have more to say than can fit in the margins, I keep a separate notebook. Whatever thoughts occur to me while I'm writing that don't fit in at the moment, that I may use later in the piece or are on a completely different topic that I'd like to save for another time, I write in another journal. I also write notes to myself in that second notebook of what I have to do later in the day so I don't keep pestering myself with the tasks' present insignificance. In addition, this extra notebook holds things I need to remember (or wish to forget) about my writing process, my life, world events as they enter my life.

A note from last week reads, "The feeling of never enough is exhausting. That's what I want to get away from. Harsh voice." I've drawn a horizontal line below that and what comes next at the bottom of the page is, "Other side of being lost is to get lost in something." "New plants" is the last thing, reminding me of my babies sitting in the sun, needing to get out of plastic and into earth. These notes are just brief clips of larger things. But when I read them, the meaning fleshes out instantly in my mind; what I've written in the notebook is what will later stimulate my thinking.

Remember nobody else has to know what you mean by these notes, they're to serve only your purposes, short is best and codes work well. A single word can send you a long way down the path. However, you don't want to engage so much in your notation that you let it take precedence over what you're developing at the time.

THE ROLE OF RITUAL IN WRITING PRACTICE

Having a specific ritual will alert your inner self that the time for writing is now. What signals can you give to your unconscious to help pave the way for creative thinking? Even the simplest rituals can help engage your mind. The child is helped into sleep each night through the repetition of small acts. He brushes his teeth and washes his face. There may be a tooth-brushing song he sings with his mother. There's a story before bed and a stuffed toy that goes under the covers up to its chin. Signals inform the mind and body of what's coming next. If you create ritual around your writing, you will support its readiness. A ritual can be a first way to invite a thing into being.

Ritual serves the writer like the chiming bells tell parishioners it's time for church. The villagers take a last sip of tea, put on their hats and coats, close their doors behind them, and walk up the hill. A writing ritual is a familiar, repeated act whose function is to alert the writer that something's changing. It's intended to set the stage for movement away from the predictable into the mystery of the unknown. It prepares the writer for internal action, reminds him that he's moving into another reality. Scholar of mythology and religion Joseph Campbell spoke about ritual this way: "One might say that the function of a ritual, and of a mythology, is to put the conscious mind—which is in touch only with the phenomenology of the world—in touch with the ground of those phenomena, particularly of your own action. So that you act not as an ego, but as a carrier of a process that is transcendent in its course. . . ." Ritual calms the conscious mind, relaxes it in a hypnotic way, as though to say, "Oh, here are the things of my life—cup, lamp, journal, yellow pencil." Those things are like a handrail on the way into the deep self.

Some writers prepare by listening to music. Music guides them into the more-than-rational world, attunes them to sound and rhythm. For others, the ritual they need is simply sharpening a dozen pencils, more than they're likely to use during the day. Ritual means the writer actually does certain things; it's based on action and belief about that action.

A number of writers wrote or spoke to me about their rituals, and here's what they said. You'll see that there's quite a range between ritual and no ritual.

Marvin Bell: "I have no rituals, but I prefer to write late at night into the wee hours when the day has passed by and the mind loosens the grip of utility and rationality. Then, emotion quickly infiltrates words. Phrases resonate more deeply. The worst aspects of the human condition seem (seem!) to be on hold."

Joseph Bruchac: "I sit down, I write."

Joy Harjo: "I prefer to write early in the morning or late at night, but the reality is that I have to write wherever and whenever I can so I've learned to write on airplanes, in hotel rooms. There is ritual, in that I pray before beginning. Often I light a candle or incense, and though I don't smoke I sometimes smoke a little tobacco.

I think of praying as talking to this creator, this creative force that is active in every cell of absolutely everything small or large. It helps. I have found that if I write at the same time every day it becomes easier to slip into the creative flow. Because I have been making my living performing, my schedule is too often erratic, but daily I do try to make time for the creative process."

Philip Levine: "I write mainly in the morning, fairly early. I might go for a two-mile walk first, I might listen to some music—Miles Davis, Bill Evans, Archie Shep, Kenny Barron. I might even read some poetry in Spanish—Machado or Garcia Lorca—or translations of Pavese or another Italian or modern Russian poet. I do those things only if nothing happens in my silence. I write with a pen, almost always the same one, an Omas, on a yellow lined pad, though a white one will do."

Carole Maso: "I will go into a sort of hypnotic, meditative zone—a position of mind, called up often by music, in order to write."

Carol Muske-Dukes: "I have no superstitions about writing, no rituals. I love that other writers do, that Alexandre Dumas père stood under the Arc de Triomphe every morning eating an apple to create orderly writing habits. I have no orderly writing habits. I write on the backs of envelopes, grocery lists—I write whenever I can cadge a minute of my own. I jump from one genre to the other."

Over time you'll create rituals that serve you. And they may not stay consistent. You may find you outgrow a particular pattern of behavior and then develop a new one to take its place. Or you may find that life intervenes in such a way that you have to adapt your writing ritual or you won't write.

When Anything Is Possible

Some writers work only at certain times of day, so the time itself becomes an indicator to get ready. In the early, early morning everything good seems possible to me. I'm talking about the time of day even before the sun's up. Once the light's come the day seems common, but before that it's like a secret. The stillness and quiet, the sense of nothing touched, nothing moving: infinite possibility. In the early morning I can become anything; the world is holy; everyone is safe. I'll take my illusion, in the moment, since it gets me to the page and allows me to open into a kind of language that later in the day my rational mind might close me off to.

The morning dark may not be the time for your writing. It may be the night that gets you going. Many writers find night to be the most secret time when they have the most freedom. If everyone's sleeping, the phone won't ring and nobody will ask anything of them. There's nowhere they have to be.

Preparing a Place

Place can be a ritual in that it offers you familiarity. Preparing a place is a way of preparing the psyche for creative work. Of this, Mary Gordon writes about her summers in Truro, Cape Cod, "One of the happiest hours of my year was the one, just after I arrived, when I unpacked the cartons of books I'd brought. I would separate the books, excited by my own discrimination like a child playing library. The purity of my categorization made me feel so blessed. Full of belief in myself, I would sit down for the first time each summer, open my notebook, and set to work." If you make a place to write, the poet within will show up. The internal critic may come along too. If you can't completely remind yourself of the importance of what you're doing, you can, at those moments, look around at the place you've made and receive comfort and inspiration from that.

Despite the grand size of my desk, its great length and its slender width, it remains phenomenally cluttered 90 percent of the time. I keep telling myself that chaos is a sign of a creative mind. I won't allow guests access to this room. I'm embarrassed by my many stacks of paper and books. I can't find bills and other important papers. Periodically I clean it off, which means I straighten my piles and stack the books I want nearby on the floor. I love to see the desk's shiny surface wiped clean of coffee cup stains, dust, and cat hair. Its cleanliness invigorates me. And yet, a few hours back at work and the desk looks like it did the day before. The thing is, it works for me this way. I guess I like to be surrounded. And in the midst of a big project it's impossible for me to give proper attention to neatness. I think my mind and soul look like this desktop.

After you've found a place—the corner of a room, a summer garden, the low-ceilinged attic, the kitchen table—consider what you want around you. I like messages—some spiritual in nature, others feisty—pasted around my computer screen and pictures on my bulletin board. The calendar from St. Frances Cabrini where I went to school as a young Catholic girl both facilitates my process and hinders it, but crooked on the wall it stays. The telephone's close by but so's the answering machine that does the talking when I don't want to. The picture of a little girl jumping is near the photo of my nephew Josh, looking very surprised over something. I feel like both those images, at various times. Find what helps you work and keep it nearby.

For Your Telling

Not only do you need a physical place but, as much of this book is about, a spiritual and holy place for your writing. It's about seeing your writing in that spiritual light and making a place within for doing your art. There's a story that the poet Wallace Stevens walked to work at Hartford Accident and Indemnity Company where he worked from 1916 until his death in 1955. On his way he stopped at a park, where he sat on a park bench and wrote poems. Once at work he'd hand his pages to his secretary who typed them up for him. The story goes that when Stevens won the Pulitzer Prize, his coworkers were surprised; they hadn't known this insurance agent was also a poet! The place he had made within himself was something his coworkers didn't know about. It was one part—a primary part—of his life.

The place we make for writing in our lives will change at times, and it will transform us. When I was in a relationship that was falling down around me and within me, I'd get out of the house before light and drive to an empty beach, park my car, drink coffee, and write before going off to teach. It got me up and out before my partner was awake. The angst I felt got written down. I think the poems lined themselves up at night in my dreams to be written in my car come morning.

The only other time I've written as much was when my mother was dying, and there was absolutely no ritual or pattern to that. Words came at every time of day and knocked against my heart and head like a woodpecker against a tree. I carried a tiny pad of paper with me everywhere I went, intent on catching each line. Difficult periods of grief or hardship often dislodge all our patterns and predictable schedules. If you can have faith in the place within, you have what's necessary for the telling to happen, no matter how the shape of the story or the walls of the place evolve.

KEEPING PROMISES

If you want to approach the untamed worlds within, you don't have to try to tame them—just show up when you say you will. In the children's story *The Little Prince*, by Antoine de Saint-Exupéry, the fox and the prince begin a friendship. When the prince comes for a second visit he's told by the fox, "It would have been better to come back at the same hour. If, for example, you come at four o'clock in the afternoon, then at three o'clock I shall begin to be happy. . . . But if you come at just any time, I shall never know at what hour my heart is to be ready to greet you. . . ."

If you intend to write each morning at eight o'clock, then keep the date with your poet within. Just like for the fox, a while before you begin to write, your imagination will begin to get ready. You may get worried too, but it's a kind of worry that propels you to work; you feel yourself getting ready for the puzzle and you want to solve it.

Your responses to keeping a schedule will vary, at times, like the Richter scale during an earthquake. You just have to show up no matter what your mind tells you, no matter the weather calling from outside. The inner weather is enough to tend to for a given amount of time each day.

COMMUNITIES OF WORDS
Writing with Others

You may find that writing in community supports your writing practice. Either by enrolling in a community college writing class, joining a privately offered workshop, or gathering with a few writing friends, the momentum created by a group may urge you on, support your new practice. Such groups become places for conversation about writing, provide opportunities to write with others, and give participants the chance to receive feedback about their work. In hearing each other's work you can see new approaches to material and inspire one another. When I'm leading groups, I present a subject or area of focus for each session and bring writing that's about the topic. We talk about the ideas, write, and then those who wish to read out loud to the group.

I encourage students to ask for the kind of response they're prepared for. If you just want to hear from others what works, then ask for that. If you only want a sounding board and no comments at all, then make that known. After a group has been together for awhile members may be more inclined to ask for and trust criticism from each other. But why take advice from someone whose opinion you may not have decided you value? Often, as we talked about in Chapter 3, the chance to read aloud and to know you're being listened to may be all you need.

At its first stage, writing, even if you're writing in the presence of others, is a private act: paper, pen, eyes, writing hand, heart, and mind. No matter the content of what's being written, the act of writing belongs to you. Journal entries, dreams, our notes in the margins of our notebooks may be meant to remain exclusive and private. We're ruminating with ourselves; it's a solely interior dialogue. But work that we develop and make into something polished deserves an audience of some kind; that is the point at which we are inclined to seek another to listen. Art is a form of communication, part of a conversation. And, however much it may be invested with the sacred realm, it's meant for other people, here and now, and maybe later. In an interview, poet Jane Kenyon said, "I want to get it public. Art isn't luxury for the privileged few, and it isn't just private. . . . It *does* matter that my work be published, made public, go into the world, and work whatever effect it has."

To make your work public doesn't have to be complicated. It can be as simple as a telephone call or a poem over tea. You may want to investigate publication through small magazines or you may choose— at first, anyway—to E-mail or send your pieces to friends. You may wish to participate in public readings sponsored by libraries, bookshops, or community centers. Often communities have "open mike" venues, where new writers can get up and read a poem or two in front of an audience. If the thought of reading for strangers is more comfortable than reading for friends, don't tell your loved ones or they may show up as a support team. When I first began reading my work publicly, I didn't want family or friends to witness my show. Now, when they come, I'm flattered.

My father used to refuse to come hear me read. I think he was afraid I'd embarrass not only him, but myself. He couldn't stand the thought. Recently, when I was invited to read an excerpt from this book at the University of California at Santa Cruz, I cajoled him into coming, promising I'd read his onion story. He didn't appear embarrassed at all and sat up near the front of the room. When we read our work in public, it changes us. The work changes too. It's the best prepublication tool for me, watching the audience's faces, hearing how the words sound outside my own room. When they fall flat, it's obvious; and when they sail, that's a happy moment.

For the Notebook 1

FUEL FOR YOUR FIRE

What fuels your writing practice? What gets you to pull up a chair and take the cap off your pen? What draws your soul to writing? Why do you think this form has chosen you? Make a list of all that inspires you. Start with the tiniest things that move you to write and go to the most grandiose: the pattern of clouds quickly sliding across summer hills, an urgency inside that repeats itself, the presence of God in your life, a compulsion to right a wrong. Welcome all the possible motivations, all your inklings toward language.

On days when you feel less than motivated to write, you may find it helpful to remind yourself of this list. Sometimes all it takes is a memory of that initial impulse. Or maybe one thing on the list will help, in the moment, to rekindle the spark within that drew you to writing in the first place.

For the Notebook 2

CREATING A RITUAL

What kind of ritual suits you? Do you want to lock the door to your room each evening after the kids are in bed and hang a No Trespassing sign from the door handle? Or do you want to bicycle to the beach in the early morning before the house wakes, before the city arises, with a thermos of tea, and find an undisturbed spot on the sand? The idea, as we've discussed, is to create actions that support what's going on within, the transformation from attention to the outer world to the inner one. The repetition of familiar actions will help you to prepare yourself.

What tools will you use? Does the pink eraser on a No. 2 pencil make it your writing utensil, or do you like that fountain pen your uncle gave you when you graduated from junior high school and its rich green ink? A number of writers I've talked to use those yellow pads with the blue lines. They're not artsy, more utilitarian, so maybe that helps you to feel that it's OK to write less than perfectly on them. I find the lines hem me in. I like to write unlined, turning the notebook on its side sometimes or writing in a few directions at once, notes in all the margins.

You might try one ritual and a particular set of tools for awhile and then try something different. You may require very few of the externals or you may need a lot of preparation to open into creativity. See what conditions support your process; do you like to write at night, in the morning? Discover how place influences both your style and content. People create under the most dire situations when they feel the necessity to do so. Establishing a ritual is a way to invite the Muse to sit beside you.

CHAPTER 7

TO PRAY IS TO LOVE

Writing and Prayer

I could make prayers or poems on and on.
Vassar Miller

Absolute attention is prayer.
Simone Weil

The essential thing is to work in a state of mind
that approaches prayer.
Matisse

"What do you pray for?" the old man selling pippins and Red Delicious asked while weighing my apples on his tipsy scale. Was he talking to someone else, I thought, looking around. But no, his eyes were on me. I repeated his question out loud to be sure I'd heard it right—not what I had expected to hear on a Tuesday afternoon downtown at the farmer's market, crowds of people everywhere. "What do I pray for? You want to know what I pray for?" I asked doubtfully, as I handed him my money, thinking about all of it—world peace, human kindness, words upon words.

The apple farmer rephrased the question. "Are you praying for redemption? Because the world's ending next week, you know." I hadn't known. "You'd best be praying," he said as he handed me my change and waved good-bye.

The world ends periodically for me. I'm often praying for it to begin again. When the words I'm hunting for don't come, no matter how hard I search, or the ones that have appeared don't seem fine enough or new enough, a piece of my world closes up, and that's a kind of ending. I ache for it to begin again, for language to open up and the words to come like so many birds entering flight. Then I pray, or I forget to pray and hold my breath, staring blankly at the gray computer screen.

At other times when I sit down at the desk and a poem's come nearly complete, as if on its own, without my doing anything, the words secure on the page before me, there's a momentary ending—a good one. For awhile I sit suspended between worlds—that of poems and that of everyday life, held by a peace that comes only after writing. My prayer is of gratitude. I wait for the *real* world to begin again, to feel my feet under me, but I'm in no hurry.

That's not what the apple farmer meant, I'm sure. The actual world didn't stop last week, at least not as far as I can tell. I wonder what ended for the farmer and if he was redeemed. From what was he delivered? Were his prayers answered?

WRITING AS PRAYER

Writing can itself be an act of prayer. Our asking for language is answered. The words come from us and from beyond us. We receive them. In *Solar Storms*, Linda Hogan writes, "I know now that the name (God) does not refer to any deity, but means simply to call out and pray, to summon. To use words and sing, to speak." This is what we do when we write; we call out. Then perhaps God is really a verb and not a noun. Maybe God is what we do when we write, breaking the order of the known and summoning language.

It may be a prayer of praise, an invocation, or a contemplative expression. The experience of writing in a state of prayer is uplifting. If I bring prayer into my practice, I feel less alone in it. And yet the writer is indwelling. It's like the whole world enters you, the boundaries between self and the external world are thinned as you receive the work. In an essay about looking at a painting, the Polish poet Zbigniew Herbert described what also could be a description of this writing state, "A suddenly awakened intense curiosity, sharp concentration with the senses alarmed, hoped-for adventure and consent to be dazzled. I experienced an almost physical sensation as if someone called me, summoned me." It can be as startling as those occasions when you look up at the sky just after a rainstorm and see corridors of light that extend brightly from the sun. You think God or some mystery is going to walk right down the ladder into town. And you're writing every rung of that ladder, whole stories and poems.

Poet Naomi Shihab Nye said, "Even as a child I felt there was this real closeness between praying and focusing on something in a way that you could write about it or trying to listen to God or to a deeper spirit in things, the way you try to listen to what images, experiences, metaphors are trying to tell you. I thought of writing as one of the ways, the kind of contemporary, long, loving look that we use when we write is very aligned with, if not identical to, the long, loving look of tradition, meditation. I think the seam is profound. They're right there together." What you offer to what you're writing is complete focus. It becomes the center of attention, the celebrated thing. In that way your subject can tell you what it has to say. Through that attention, everything else fades away and it's like you're a diviner, using all your skill and knowledge to find water.

I've been watching the NBA play-offs. What most intrigues me about the games is the quality of attention that these guys have. There's Kobe Bryant about to make a free throw. The Lakers are nine points behind. The music in the Staples Center is blaring loudly and there's a horn tooting. The fans are shouting and waving bright yellow sticks in the air. But the look on twenty-one-year-old Bryant's face is of concentration. He looks intent but calm. It's just him and the basketball. The room's distractions seem lost on Bryant. The man is focused. He has entered the zone.

Sometimes the feeling that occurs when writing is a trancelike mood that's so strong, I don't think I can contain it; I think I will catch fire from the heat of the light. It's as though there's actual current running out my fingers onto the computer keys. Then I get up and throw cold water on my face, look in the mirror a moment and say, "Eyes, nose, ears, lips." I need to remember the physical and clearly definable. But I don't stay away too long because the words are my fuel and, ultimately, I want that divine fire.

You won't find the writing state of prayer on any map. It's not in the heavy atlas you first looked at as a child at your grandma's knee. She might have said, "We come from here," pointing to a pink shape with a many-syllable name. But the state of prayer is a place nonetheless, in and not in the body, as what your grandmother pointed to was in the atlas but more truly something else that you could barely imagine.

THE STATE OF PRAYER

To enter the place of prayer doesn't require fancy equipment. It's about, as we discussed in the first chapter, the place where you live and being there. When words are coming directly from my spiritual self,

I feel present to the deep life, the inner workings—not only of my individual self but of the world, at least a bit of it. At those times I feel like a messenger or a scribe. I'm writing what's being told to me. What has gotten me there? Asking. If you ask for the mystery and the gift of language you will receive.

It can be difficult to go somewhere unfamiliar without clear directions, maps, and guides. We often want the specific steps. While working with a group, one of the participants asked me, "What does it look like when you're writing in a state of prayer? I want to see it. Can you show it to me?"

Here's a picture. A writer sits down in her room or in a corner of the kitchen when no one else is there. She has performed the rituals that signify to her that time is changing, the mood is altering, the expectations are not those based on end products and the finished thing. She's got her journal on her lap or paper stacked on the table, a pen in her hand. She might read the words of others to remind her that the world of poetic thought is less linear than that of much of daily life.

She's not, at the moment, preparing something for someone else. It may get there. It may end up a story in a book. But for now that's not the objective. A story published in a book is later, another thing entirely. What matters now is this time, this breath of time spreading out on the table before her. And though it may, in reality, be that she has one hour to be here, in the space she's creating inside herself the moment is without limit. It is vast and open and hers. That's the state of prayer, the frame of mind she's entering.

Her attention moves from outward concerns—the doctor's appointment in the afternoon, the bills yet to be paid—to inward awareness. It's not that the outside concerns go away; it's that they're incorporated into the inward space as a piece but not the whole. They blend with the colors and shapes and memories that make the pattern of her thought. Not thought only, but also sensory awareness, feelings, vague inklings.

To pray is to love, to love the moment, the thing she's writing about. One of the gifts of writing is to love; it brings her to more and more love the more she writes. Just to give herself the time is an expression of love. So if you were to walk into the kitchen and see her there, you might see a woman touching paper, fingers on her pen, eyes cast softly out the window. It might not be obvious but you would witness a woman loving. You might not see much of anything out of the ordinary. But what you couldn't see are the workings inside her and her attention drawing inward, blending daily life, world events, the past and the future, the smells of the room and more—all that is particular to this writer on this morning in this room. In art, as in any spiritual practice, it helps if you bring your whole self to it. No part of you is unnecessary. Even the parts you'd prefer to do away with at other times belong here and now.

When you sit down remember this: what you write doesn't have to be true in a literal sense. It may contain images, ideas from various sources, some actual, some imagined. The connections between the sentences may not be clear as you're writing. Your job is to accept and write them down. What you write doesn't have to make logical sense any more than a prayer has to make perfect sense. If you try to edit during the prayerful inception stage, you'll close off the channel.

You can't expect your words to be completely clear from the get-go. Give yourself time to find your way. Short periods of writing may be what's best at first. Sit quietly, shift your awareness from solely the outer world and daily responsibilities to an inward-outward, open attention. Notice how big the inner place of awareness can be.

Remember that the experience may not be extraordinary. No trumpets blare, and angels won't come down from the sky. A velvet carpet doesn't lead the way from the outer life to the writing life. To write in a state of prayer is to enter an elevated awareness that's available to ordinary human beings, whether you can walk over hot coals barefoot or not. What you write is made out of the ordinary. The ordinary with a twist. The fiber of your work comes from the material world. Stories are made by hand. They're made from tables and chairs, fears and jealousies, what you had for breakfast, the desired and undesired ring of the telephone, a letter in the mail marked "urgent."

KEEPING THE CHANNEL OPEN

There is a vitality, a life-force, an energy, a quickening that is translated through you. . . . You have to keep the channel open.

MARTHA GRAHAM

One December a few years ago, I sat with a friend of mine who was dying. Her extended group of friends and family sat shifts twenty-four hours a day, so that Rosmarie would be well attended and could remain at home where she wanted to be, loved and cared for. During the first weeks we watched Charlie Chaplin movies and Rosmarie laughed. The nearer she got to passing, she became aware of things one ordinarily isn't conscious of. She knew when the phone was going to ring before it did and who would be on the other line. "My brother's calling from Switzerland," she said right before he did. Or she'd say, "Susan's at the front door," and though there'd been no knock before she spoke, there was one now. Her channels were wide open to what was of this world and the world beyond. As she transitioned to the next, her awareness became unusually keen. In keeping the channel open, writers do that, they know what they couldn't with it closed.

A few days after Rosmarie died I went up to the wintry hills northwest of Sacramento where writing comes to me with the least effort. A poem prayed its way to the surface, and I wrote. I was trying to piece together what I'd experienced with her. It ends with this stanza:

> *How do you die, let go of what is known, the familiar?*
> *How do you open the shutters and allow the wind inside,*
> *the whole cold wind, let it in? Doorway, path,*
> *black church steeple outside the window*
> *and the bells chime on Sunday.*
> *She will walk the tributaries, fingerings of water*
> *past where the river divides, up the frosted*
> *northern slope, glacial blue,*
> *the underside.*

To write it, I had simply to move aside, get out of my own way, and listen to the larger, more significant voice that knows I can do more than I usually think I can. The words came till they were finished coming. It was obvious when that was; there was a sound and then there was no sound. I was in a receptive state and knew the words that were coming to me were not entirely mine. I couldn't dictate and direct them. I aligned myself with not only my spiritual self, but the spiritual essence of everything, and then the words came.

Moving out of prayer, I saw the poem had elements to work with and later I brought in my more ordinary, commonplace, and logical way of thinking to put the poem into shape. It didn't take much tinkering, just some fine-tuning was all. Prayer can bring us to our greatest knowing. Spiritual energy, to use Graham's words, is "translated through you."

No Trespassing

What paralyzes me is when the No Trespassing sign is in front of me in bright red. It means "writing's closed," as though the way to my words is a road covered in snow and temporarily impassable. I'm bewildered as to how to get in. Can I leave my car behind and sneak through chinks in the gate? Will I freeze in all that snow?

At those times, the poet within is silent. "Unh, unh," she says, "I'm not going to give you words. You want too much." She's right, I do. I've always been that way. How about you? How much do you want and what has writing got to do with it?

The prayer I have when words are blocked is an asking prayer. I'm not very good at praying. Sometimes I lose interest in the prayer before one go-round. Or I forget the words. I want the results, damn it, *now*. Give me those words I've been hunting for. My prayer might simply sound like this: "Dear Poetry, please give me my words back. Show me that other side where I speak freely and words come with ease. Please remove the shackles from my mind so that I can find my voice again." But the other prayer that might serve me well would be the prayer of acceptance.

Acceptance is so often the first step to change. It's not that I have nothing to say, it's that I can't find it because of all the cotton in my brain and heart. Often, it's a short-lived experience and if you can accept it, you'll find your words just on the other side. We'll talk in depth about fallow times and the strife and richness those times can bring us in the next chapter.

These days I want heartfelt, precise words and sentences and paragraphs and chapters to come at my beck and call. The poet within says, "You've got to pray. What has happened to your patience? Did you accidentally toss it in the trash with your pencil shavings?" She says some of the things I might say to you. I mutter prayers to myself, having lost faith in my poet for the moment.

Since I've always been a sufferer and come from a family of them, maybe that's just the way it's going to be for me. I will sometimes rage against myself, mean as a hungry dog on a short leash, and be in need of prayer and celestial (or other) intervention. As we discussed in Chapter 5, that's the rub, and writing can come out of that struggle. The lively, alert impulse to write pushes against the part of the self that holds back from expression, is fearful or distrusting of it.

Praying can help to bring me back to myself, back to true acceptance, the part of my self not built on deadlines and commitments to the outside world, the shy poet part, the playfully writing a story part. In his book *Be Careful What You Pray For*, Larry Dossey writes, "We don't fully trust prayer, perhaps because it invokes powers that we feel cannot be understood and controlled. Our ambivalence toward prayer is embedded in our language. For instance, our word *deprecate*, meaning to belittle someone, is related to the Latin root of prayer, *precarius*." Yes, writing can be a precarious endeavor and you might tend to deprecate your work. It may be helpful to remember that your hesitation toward writing and prayer aren't just individual but are part of our language and culture. Yet, aren't many of the best things in life chancy? Standing on the narrow branch of the writing life, precarious as it can be, is where we get the goods. It's only there that our words take wing.

BENEFITS OF PRAYER

In this week's issue of the free local newspaper, the Question Man asked several people whether prayer works. Each of the respondents replied similarly, "I think it makes me feel better." You may think prayer's supposed to do more than make you feel better. But isn't that an important step to healing? And when it comes to writing, if finding the words to a prayer is the closest you can come at the moment to your novel, and you feel better, aren't you closer to writing that big story? When comforted by prayer, you get more of your possible self back; you're engaging your deepest belief and associating with mystery. More than just feeling good can come from prayer, but feeling better will facilitate your writing.

Prayers can infuse a writing practice with light, put space around it, and breath. They slow things down. So that instead of rushing ahead into the whirlwind of what you might write, hope you can write, are afraid you can't write, you're in the present moment, which is in fact where the words will eventually come from. They may be about the past or the future, but when they hit the paper it's now. Fast praying doesn't count; skipping over the words and their meaning is more like playing hopscotch in a hurry than anything blessed. The idea of a prayer is to sink into its words, to pay attention to them. You actually say one word at a time.

Prayer can help give you patience. And when it comes to writing, patience is a very important thing. The slow moments of being with the words in front of you will alter your perception of time. The spiraling of trying to get somewhere stops. Patience comes out of faith, the faith you put in the words of the prayer as you slowly give yourself to them. The poet Rainer Maria Rilke said, "Be patient toward all that is unsolved in your heart and try to love the questions themselves."

To pray is to ask. It's a meek thing to do. You admit you want. To ask is to say you need and you don't have. You're asking for words. If I can get myself into that place of asking, answers do arrive—not necessarily to the question I'd posed, but ultimately the one I most needed answered. In the children's book *Mrs. Frisby and the Rats of NIMH,* Robert C. O'Brien writes, "All doors are hard to unlock until you have the key." When it comes to writing, prayer may be your key.

To feel turned away from language is hardly the only reason to include prayer in your writing practice, but like with the rest of life, desperation is often what brings us to our knees. Praying can bring you to the place of the essential voice, your home. At times that's the only way I can get there. I want to speak with the voice unclouded, and prayer reminds me it's not so far away; it doesn't have to be fancy, or prettier and smarter than I am.

Do I want redemption, like the born-again apple farmer? I think so. Looking over the dictionary definition of *redeem,* I know I want poetry to redeem me, to give me back my value when I fear it's fallen away, to prove to me that words are where I come from, that they align me with my source. I want to buy back, or "ransom," not my innocence as the dictionary says, but words. If there were such a deal as one good line of poetry in trade for a night of sleep, I'd take it. However, I don't want to be faultless. Faults work into my writing and I need them. They urge me on and show me not only where I've written less well, but often a secret that actually strengthens the work because in its awkwardness it's new. The fault may show me a surprising way to go. Faults keep me new and learning.

I do want to be set free or saved, not as a sinner, but as a writer. Prayer can set you free, at least temporarily. I ask to be saved from hesitation, exhaustion, the pain in my right shoulder. I ask to be set free from staid, reliable language and lifted into the startling.

Invocation

What do you wish to have in your writing life? Can you ask for it? When you invoke something, you call on it, call for it. It's a declaration of need and desire. To invoke implies asking beyond the self. You're putting yourself out there, declaring your request. The poet Rumi wrote, "You must ask for what you want. Don't go back to sleep." If you don't ask, your desire for words will remain hidden under everything else you do.

Incantations and chants are ways of asserting and invoking. In the early eighties, affirmations were the rage, at least where I was. Many people were writing them. The idea was to make positive, declarative statements about what you wanted to be true but weren't convinced of. By using your mind and writing them down, time after time, the statements—or at least your belief in them—would become real. If you bring your belief together with your writing in the form of incantations and chants, change will occur. Invocation is a very powerful tool. The affirmations I wrote nearly twenty years ago did assist me in making change. The lines don't do it by themselves. Even with the aid of belief, I found action was required, or such deep belief as to connote action.

PRAYER AS A WAY OF GIVING THANKS

To give thanks is to recognize what has come to you. First there was the empty page and now there's something on it. When you give thanks, your gratitude is what you give back to the Great Spirit in recognition of a gift received. You give your regard for what you've created. You could have just as easily—and sometimes more easily—not received that thing. You could have looked the other way, not taken the invitation. Your paper would be blank.

How does the seed give thanks? It flowers. You take what you have, who you are, and you respond to the gift of that beingness with a course of action that aligns with it. You do what is in your nature. If you're called to write, you feel the need for words and stories; this is your nature. If it is your nature, it is your right. Many of us are further from our true natures than the grasshopper is from his; we often try to fit where we don't fit, work at jobs we don't like, live in cities when we wish we lived in the country. Since we have will and choice and self-doubt, how do we determine our natures? I think it's a matter of following the soft voice within, listening to the place it issues from, and supporting it as we can.

It's easy to say, "Well, I've got that paragraph, but it isn't much." It may never be enough by some standard of perfection that you walk around with for whatever reason. If you keep yourself in the place of "not enough," then you'll continue to disavow the gift, however small, that you have received.

The author Joseph Bruchac said, "The only time I find doubt or dissatisfaction coming into my writing or my life is when I forget to be thankful—thankful for even the smallest gifts. As soon as I remember that, the doubt and dissatisfaction vanish." When I read this, I decided to try it. No matter how little or how much I'd written, no matter what fault I could see in it, after a day of writing I gave thanks. It worked. The way I viewed what I'd written and the way I viewed myself and my recognition of the spirit's role in my work were all influenced positively. When I give thanks for whatever comes, the writing goes in deeper and settles there. There's more love inside me then and my soul feels seen, not slandered. Now, each day, before I begin, while I'm writing and afterward, I give thanks for the work. It's made all the difference.

If you can accept what is given, you help to create an internal and external environment of receptivity. Then the spiritual force of creativity has somewhere to go, as though you give it something to adhere to. Much of creativity concerns being receptive to what's around you—the images, sounds, moods, interactions, keeping every cell of your body alert and open.

It might be helpful to consider it this way. Think about someone who has extended himself or herself for you and how you feel about that person. What's the emotion of gratitude like for you? Where does it come from? Where in your body do you feel it? Might you be able to offer that to yourself, to your words, and to the place they've come from?

And when your paper remains blank, can you give thanks for that as well? That's much harder for me. Because I see myself as that blank and empty space. This sends me off on an old, spiraling-into-the-dark-hole direction where I'd prefer not to go. If I could reframe the idea of blank as the yet-to-be something instead of nothing, that might help. Or to simply remove the negative value placed on nothing would greatly relieve me of the downward spiral. Admittedly, I'm not there yet. I like the idea of giving thanks for what is even when it's emptiness, and the idea of giving thanks for what is not yet. It is a new thing to bring into my practice as I continue on in my writing life.

For the Notebook 1

TAKE TEN

Ten minutes, that is. Ten minutes when you don't have anything else you've got to do, nowhere else you've got to be, those ten minutes that float between one thing and the next, a moment of slow breaths taken. If you have to get up really early to do this, do it. Then sit in a quiet room with the bright lights turned down. Open your notebook, let your attention be on all the reasons you ought not be here, all the things you've got. Make a list of them, but don't try to work things out or future plans. Let your eyes move as they will, touching and recording whatever you happen to notice. Begin writing with what you see or with what you hear.

We tend to think that poems and stories require more than we have to give them in ten minutes. Well, they do and they don't. Beautiful writing doesn't have to be made out of something you don't have. You have what it requires whether, at the moment, that's a small story or a large one.

You might like to start your writing off by asking. It's amazing what a request can bring. Asking tends to bring answers. Whom do you want to ask: God, the Great Spirit, the roots of an old tree where they spread far into the earth? Ask for words and to be invited into the place words come from, the place of prayer.

Whatever you write, do so without self-judgment. After all, these are the words you asked for. If you begin to be judgmental, imagine your internal critic small beside you with something else to do. You may have to repeat this step over and over to get to the point of writing without criticism. Then again, the words may rush to the paper, fearless.

After you've written for those ten minutes, read what the paper's got, noticing how you respond to your own words. You might read it a second time out loud. The idea is to read and notice your response, just acknowledge it.

For the Notebook 2

WORDS TO PRAY

There are prayers for rain and for world peace, prayers before supper, matins, or morning prayers. Often the prayers we say are those we learned as children. Even if they're prayers we've learned more recently, they're exactly that, learned, memorized words written by somebody else.

How about writing your own prayers? What would they be for? A prayer for writing? A thanksgiving prayer to say after having been blessed by words? Or a prayer for the roots of the tree that sends ideas for poems your way? A prayer to the critic within, without a mean word anywhere?

To write a prayer, begin by asking for the words and see what comes. Write your prayer word by word. Give it time. Then try saying it. If your tongue stumbles somewhere or gets stuck on words, look at that part again and see what you might want to change, what is being told to you. Maybe there's more to say here. Listen for the sounds and how certain sounds might repeat, resembling your heartbeat, becoming the chorus of the prayer, if you wish to write it that way.

You might put your prayer away for a few days and come back to it later to see what's there. Have the words somehow changed in your absence? Play with what you have and consider it an adventure to see where you end up. The prayer itself, when it's complete, may turn out to be no more than five lines, a dozen words. But expect anywhere from five to ten pages in order to get down to the essence, which is what both prayer and poetry are. Write it big, read it over, and take what shines. Then do it again. You might find it fruitful to make a list of all the words, phrases, and sentences that, when you read it over, attract you. You may find you're writing more than one prayer.

CHAPTER 8

WORDLESSNESS IN
WRITING PRACTICE
Absence and Longing

What is hidden is more real than what is manifested.
Simone Weil

I love the dark hours of my being in which
my senses drop into the deep.
Rainer Maria Rilke

in longing you close your eyes
Myra Shapiro

L onging fuels both writing and spiritual life. It's what gets you to the page and brings you to your knees. Longing to write can grab you when you're sweeping the floor or driving to work. It's that yearning for words to describe and define, to find expression and form, to hold mystery and to root it in tangible words.

One of my writing students said, "When I'm longing to write, nothing else interests me. I don't want to eat or talk. I do what I have to do to maintain life's order, but what I want is to sit down at my desk and listen for what's trying to be said. Once I'm there, the words at first approach like timid animals and then more quickly." The Indian poet Mirabai turned her longing for God into devotional poems and, like Kabir and Rumi, spoke of Him as a lover or friend:

> *Friend, I have lost all sleep.*
> *I spend the whole night*
> *Watching and waiting for the Beloved.*
> *My companions came to lecture me,*
> *But my mind would not listen.*
> *Without seeing Him I cannot rest . . .*

In the elevated state of longing, rest is difficult to get. To desire stories and poems is like desiring God. Both yearnings are based on faith and need, and as such require love, patience, and commitment. If you don't feel a need for language, you won't write.

If you give yourself to your devotion, to your longing, to the mystery of soul made manifest through language, you'll find the way toward words opens. The writing comes. The words find you because you've made yourself ready for them, have stayed with the longing and not fled from it.

HOW CAN I MISS YOU?

In writing practice, as in much of life, the old adage "How can I miss you, if you won't go away?" applies. Reading Stacy Schiff's biography of Véra Nabokov, it seems this didn't apply to her husband, Vladamir Nabokov. His writing habits could make many of us feel like slouches. He was always working on at least one book, or a book and a short story, or translations of his work. Even during his butterfly-catching sojourns, he'd write when not out on the trail with his net. Most writers I know aren't like that. The well needs to be replenished and it takes time for it to fill. Whether time away from writing is self-imposed or just the way life is for a period, whether it's pleasant or dreadful and lonely, I've found that absence from writing and the longing to get back to it are essential to my writing life. They deepen it, invite the rough edges of life and soul and heartache into the practice. The nuances and cracks and questions that are part of living an examined life churn around within and will influence the work when I return to it. The longest I've ever gone without writing is six months or so. Following that silence, when the writing flows again, it's been altered in some ways. Transformation occurred while my pen was still.

At the end of a writing project or the last page in a journal, during a bout of writer's block, or because the intervention of another aspect of life supersedes the writing, absence from it makes the heart for words grow fonder. The worst part of extended periods of not writing, particularly when you feel blocked off from language, is the intense fear that the writing's gone and will never ever come back. I've felt that many times. It can be awful and bitter, harder than a door slammed in my face. It's odd, for I held a pen in my hand and produced poems only a month ago, but if for a few weeks or months I can't find the right words, I'm convinced that I will never again be able to write anything other than grocery lists. Suddenly I'm not who I was; my name doesn't fit me. And I don't like this person, don't even want to be in the same room as her. I see myself as fraudulent. If during one of those times I'm invited to give a reading of my work, I hesitate to accept because I feel the inner poet has abandoned me, so whose work would I be reading? I'm sad, fearful, angry that I was given the gift I'd always wanted and then some evil force snatched it away.

Luckily, wending it's way beside those emotions is also persistent longing, an ache powered by a desire so strong that it feels like it comes from outside of my body. The essence of creativity, the source that we can drop down into at times, feeds my spring. Even if I'm shut off to it, that imaginal world is still active within. Dreams prove it to me. They don't stop when the writing does. It's just that I've hit the pause button. Longing is a form of grace. I am graced by desire to make meaning with words on paper. It's something God gives me out of his love for my bit of creating. We are, by nature, creative beings. The longing to be so is also a part of our nature.

In an essay called "The Little Bit," which appeared in my anthology *Storming Heaven's Gate: An Anthology of Spiritual Writings by Women*, Gene Zeiger writes, "Because of the little bit that isn't there, that life refuses to bring; . . . because of that tiny bit of space, that little absence, I once felt a longing so intense it made me cry. . . ." When we experience longing, it isn't just for words that we're aching, it's for that little bit, our essence, the primal stuff the soul is made of.

You long for what may be. That keeps you going, keeps you seeking the next idea. Longing defines inspiration. You desire enlightenment, to see through this to that, for an answer you can rely on. When desiring to write, you admit your need and dedication, and put yourself at the service of your art, your love, your God. You're at the mercy of what you do not have (the next story or poem). You hope it exists but it isn't in your grasp.

Longing can be like a drug in the strong way it can affect us. When my husband leaves town, I often want him to go, despite the fact that I adore him. I like to be alone, and thrive on days and days of it. My writer-self needs solitude. It supports my writing and my loving. (We'll talk more about solitude in the writing process in Chapter 10.) Having time alone makes me a kinder person. The nights Michael's away I sleep in one of his shirts and long for his return. He's gone; I want him gone; but I long for him to return. It's not that the grass is always greener, but that the state of longing is a fruitful state of being, whether it's love for poetry or a human being. To be without gives us an opportunity to romanticize the other, to idealize and also to catch glimpses of it at a distance. The mountains appear quite different from afar than they do close up. I look at the climb from miles away and think, piece of cake. Once the car is parked at the foot of the path, that walk is another matter, and I may feel daunted by the incline and by how far it is to the top. There are two poems there, the one I get from being nearby and the one I can only get from a distance, where miles, sunlight, fog, and memory influence what I see in a muted way. I long for both those poems.

When I'm finished writing this book, I may wish to be wordless for awhile. I'm loving writing more than I love a lot else, but it's hard work cranking out words every day. If I told you I long for writing at this pace to go on forever, I'd be lying. I look forward to being on the other side of a big project for a spell. Knowing my process as I do, give me a few weeks of semiwordlessness (I'm nearly never without my notebook and notes to friends, as well as assorted E-mail messages), and I'll be begging to write again. Poetry, I think. After this year of prose, that's where I'm headed, into the hooded, semidarkness of that world. A longing for poems is in me now, but I can't indulge it; I can't let myself stray from the path of this book. So even while in the writing, we can long for it. It's a luxury to simultaneously long for something and have it.

In an essay in *The New Yorker* titled "On Impact," Stephen King writes about having been hit by a car while walking along a country road. The accident nearly killed him and the healing process took a long time, during which he was in awful pain. He hadn't written for five weeks when he began to consider getting back to writing. He had a sense that since writing had helped him in the past, it could again. He heard a voice at the back of his mind urging him on. King writes, "It was possible for me to disobey that voice but very difficult not to believe it." That voice calls the writer part of the self when the time has come to be back at work. It's like an insistent tapping on your shoulder. Then you know the absence is over for now and you return. For me, it's like becoming whole again. You can't know what will come out of sitting down with your work, but you can know that something will. Until that time, the longing may present itself to you at every turn.

The Other Self

When we feel driven away from our work, we're longing for our other self, the poet within. As Carol Muske-Dukes writes, "There is always the sense one has, in writing, of apprehending one's 'double'—the other identical self who is free of conventional thinking and idealized and moving as fast as thought can move." It's the shadow-self that couldn't balance a checkbook if it tried. When we're active in the external realms, that wild, spontaneous thinker may not be invited into our lives and goes into hiding. Then we long for it. Sometimes it comes out in dreams, trying to hit us over the head with images we'll notice as a call to writing. It's not solely the act of writing that we long for, but that aspect of our being.

Once I dreamed I killed myself, or rather, I killed one of my selves, because part of me was still very much alive. In the dream I was trying to figure out how to dispose of my body, my other body. I didn't want it to be found and if it were, I certainly didn't want it to be identified as me. I considered cutting off its hands so my fingerprints wouldn't reveal my identity. It was gruesome. I woke up shivering, rubbing my hands together.

To be without hands would make it impossible to write. To be without fingerprints is to be without identity. The dream is about cutting myself off from my double—the creative, inspired self. This misdeed implies fear of the complicated, inner life. The layers of that life overwhelm me at times. There are times I pull back, cut myself off from them. I'm thankful for the dream that brought the workings of my soul to the surface and thankful also that in the dream I had contemplated the action and not taken it. If I cut myself off from my other, then who am I?

THE DESIRE TO BE FREE OF LONGING

Your desire to fill pages with writing makes it your promise, your work, and your love. Each word must be made of a portion of awareness, thought, feeling, so that phrases will be strung together like a chain, linked by commas and periods. You're counting on the words, and you are afraid of being empty.

At times we want to be free of longing. It's sticky! To desire the invisible is difficult. How do you know for certain when you've got it in hand? But if you deny longing you just shut yourself down. If you say, "Forget it, writing's too hard a master to follow, it's so unpredictable," but you're called to write and really do want to, then it's like closing a door to the wealth of soul.

Neglected Longing

Many people who want to write never pick up the pen. They long for it, sometimes for years, but keep themselves from it. Chances are that you've accepted the invitation to write, or are ready to, if you're reading this book.

My student Linda writes: "This deep longing, I fear it like Hurricane Floyd. . . . It's time to evacuate, take only what you can carry, your children . . . into a new land you hope you will recognize." It feels like the longing may whisk you away as though you're in the path of a hurricane. Will following it cause you to lose sleep, abandon your family, lose the sense of form you've given your life? Yes and no. To follow your longing into writing you will be changed, but not so drastically that you'll give up the entire life you've made for yourself. Writing's not going to lead you astray. But if you deny your desire for the heart of words, you may then find yourself feeling lost and cut off from your spiritual self. If you follow the essential self into words, you only deepen and expand. Ramona, a new student to my workshop, writes, "My desire to write is insatiable. Can I bear it? How do I hold it?" It's through the telling the longing is born and carried.

Neglected longing, fed by self-doubt, can keep us away from writing. We think we want the answer but we're afraid we may not like the one we write. Does the longing feel too big to be written? It's not. If you approach writing one phrase at a time and seek guidance and accompaniment when you need it, it likely won't overwhelm you. I play that old "What's the worst thing that could happen?" game with myself sometimes. The worst thing is usually something like, "I might write really badly." I have many times. But when I've failed, the floor hasn't opened up and sent me to bad writer's hell. I've just felt frustrated and lonely that I couldn't get to the words that would meet me.

You need to know that some days you lose, you write really horrible, sloppy, soppy stuff; but then there are days when the words shine and everything you've lost becomes worth these words you've just found. What distinguishes the writer from the hobbyist is that the writer writes anyway, despite the less-than-good days. To stay in the practice, present with the fear of not getting to the heart of the matter, keeps you on the edge, an edge as pointed as a sharp pencil's lead. If you disavow and malign the longing, you may not long any less, but you'll be frustrated and angry. If you can, say, "I long for what I do not have," and then write what you do not have. Or write what you do have. Write whatever it is you long for. Take the ache and make it the substance by writing it down word for word. It's painful at times, but at least you don't neglect your longing, which can feel like giving up breathing. If you were to cut yourself off from your longing, how would you recognize who you are? To write from the soul is not to deny but to embrace.

WHAT DO YOU LONG FOR?

What do you long for? Is it what's gone or what you're hidden from? So often deep desire is about more than one thing. Writing embraces that. It takes you just as you are. You know the ache of longing and may try to pin it on this or that, but no one thing holds. The soul embraces the many answers over the singular easy one.

When writing, begin with the thing itself, rather than an analysis of it. You might try thinking of writing as the ripples of water on a pond after a rock's been thrown in. Initiate your writing with the arc of your throwing arm sending a stone into the water. Splash, the rock goes down. Write the ripples that move concentrically outward. Notice how the language is there if you start small and slow, writing moment by moment. You cannot know the end of what you'll write till you get there, just like you can't know the end of any particular longing until you come to completion, either through living it out or through writing.

If you're aware of an indiscriminate sense of longing, writing is a way to bring it into focus. What feels disparate and unruly will begin to find form and substance. When the paper's got hold of a phrase, your mind can let it go and another will come forward, each further delineating the feeling. Soon you'll find you have a portrait of it.

LONGING IN CREATIVE WORK

A sense of longing may be present when you are actually engaged in writing and when you are not. When I'm writing at my desk, I'm in a state of mind that contains longing. I desire to tell the story well, to find the next thought, for the language to surprise me and to say what I've never said before. I'm craving more of what I'm having at the moment. It's a greedy feeling. I want another miracle, another testament that out of longing something will come from the mystery.

The poet and children's book author Pat Mora said, "I have to mull a bit. I'm fishing sometimes for a line, sometimes it's a concept . . . that will let me in. . . . You're always trying to listen. . . . I'm casting about." There's a longing for what the fishing line will bring up, a curiosity fueled by longing and the chance of failure, fear that the story may be unattainable. You wait for what's invisible because before the words, the sense of what you want to say is invisible. The energy of the room is filled with expectancy.

It's easy to just sit there thinking about what you could write. But to work with the longing that motivates you and use it like gasoline to fuel the process, you have to coax it onto the page, keep pace with it. Listen for what's true. Bring your evaluating mind in later.

At times I feel the longing to write and then while I'm at it, I'm overcome by questions about the work. It's distracting, not helpful to what I'm doing. There's the internal critic interfering again, wanting to stop the exploration, to void my curiosity and natural impulses. I find it necessary to distinguish between the writing itself and my feelings about what I'm doing. If you can say to yourself, "This is the work; those are the feelings," it helps. To see them as separate will help you to keep the pencil moving, and support your longing and desire to write.

Often in writing a sense of longing comes up when we're working on really big ideas, when we're trying to express what we haven't fully formed as thought yet. I'm referring to prethought, what's known but not fully, cognitively recognized. It may be the ineffable or it may be that which has not yet crystallized. Since we are this assemblage of past, present, future, personal self, spiritual self, and the world that affects us, there's often much going on internally. We long to express it but don't quite know how. "I'm trying to say what I don't know how to say," a student tells me in a panic over the phone. "Start with any one word," I tell her. "I promise it will be the right one." She doubts me and asks how I know. I tell her it's because you can't know anything else, because if you doubt yourself at every pass, you'll write nothing and stay in the ache of longing. I know because I don't believe your inner wisdom would desert you, even when you desert yourself.

THE FALLOW TIMES

If you haven't already, at some point you'll acquaint yourself with the I'm-Not-Ready-to-Speak place. In the midst of a family, community, or world crisis you may find your writer's voice gone from you. Or, for no obvious reason, the tendency toward language remains out of reach. You look for words everywhere—under rocks, in the medicine cabinet, in the piles of paper on your desk—and find none that belong to you. You can only utter the same few syllables over and over again. Within, you find no substance, message, or impulse that moves you to write. You can't force the language; or maybe you can, but for a spiritual writing life it's not usually fruitful to do so.

At times writing isn't possible, it's not the right thing to do because something else is going on in your psyche. You're sifting, sorting, weighing life. You're slogging through the mud in heavy boots and can't step back yet to write about it. When you're in the midst of experience and wholly giving yourself to it, that's all you can do. There are other periods when reflection is what's called for and to write would be premature. The soul's yearning at these times is not to speak. It requires silence. To put pen to paper would be to move against your inner wisdom. It's natural to need a rest from forming words, sentences, and paragraphs. To rest is not to be vacant; to rest is to replenish. Not every time is right to make something. We all go through times of emptiness or just silence.

The compulsive aspect of the doing-self may tell you to "do something." Our current preoccupation with more activity, more making, finding, expanding, developing, and so on implies that we're worthwhile only if we're doing. The tangible results aren't all that counts in a writer's life. Often what's most interesting is what we cannot see. If you're going to write authentically, you'll need to tend the silence as well as the words. It's a myth that writers are always productive.

Writers write when they're not actually at their desks, during the fallow periods as well as during the times when pages are being produced. When you're doing the dishes, or putting a tired child to bed, or building a fence, you may also be writing. From the outside, when we're engaged in reflection, thought, and prayer it appears we're doing nothing. It is during these times that novels are conceived. This is work; it's just that it's invisible work. We may not know a novel is percolating during a fallow season. We just know we're not writing and that we feel lousy about it.

At those times, I'm miserable. I don't look good or feel right. My hair is the wrong hair; my humor's gone flat; nobody laughs at my jokes. The food I cook is dull and tasteless. My thoughts bore me. My love notes stink. I feel barren, like nothing is happening within me, certainly nothing that would lead to a decent poem. I feel cut off during those times, less than myself.

This is the writer's void. I don't think there's a way for it to be pleasant. If you want to delve into the spiritual heart of the writing life, you're going to encounter fallow periods and you're probably not going to feel good when you do. You'll feel your grief, not just about your lack of writing but perhaps other sorrows that come forward. You sense your loss and longing. If you can open yourself to those feelings, see the gift of their natures, the grief will in time find words.

Wordlessness is a part of the process of writing authentically and deeply. You have to suffer these periods and go into the void where you will feel sorrow and pain. Maybe not every writer goes there, though most do. I haven't spoken to a writer whose work I love that writes nonstop, all the time, without a disruption of the flow. Simone Weil knew that "not to exercise all the power at one's disposal is to endure the void." It's like holding your finger to the flame instead of pulling it away. Can you allow the absence of language to be rather than to fill the void with various distractions?

If you can open your awareness this way, you'll see that a writing life isn't just what happens on the page, it's made of everything that leads up to that point. That includes your own emptiness. Out of that void comes grace. It may take weeks or months. Some artists go years without producing anything. You don't even have to have faith. There are even times we need to not have faith. When we're without faith we've hit rock bottom. That level of despair can be an important part of the process. It's real. Even the most faithful lose their faith at times. To acknowledge an absence of faith is to tell the truth. You don't see a way out and, as a result, really experience the void. Robert Frost said, "The best way out is always through." It's the only way out, really.

The Richness of the Void

After harvesting the last of their summer vegetables my friends Sue and Steve, organic gardeners in the foothills of the Sierra, plant a cover crop of fava beans to winter over the ground. They don't sow them to eat but because the plants will supply needed nitrogen to the ground, which will enhance the next crop of vegetables they'll take to market. They won't need to tend this earth until early spring. During the winter, the beans and the soil will do their work together. Sometimes you set the stage and then just let things happen.

The unseen happenings underground are a kind of magic, the roots wending their way down. They press and tuck and sink into the earth. When you are away from words and feel lost to the manifestation of your spirit, your own roots are twisting their way down so that, when the light shines again, you'll have firmer ground to stand on, a surer place to draw your soulful words from.

What helps me to get through wordless times is to remember that the writing is working in me during these periods. After nearly every fallow period I've gone through, when I've begun writing again, there's been an increase to the work. It has more depth, the subjects coming through are new, the style has shifted in one way or another—I'm suddenly writing long narrative poems, or I find myself working with a particular movement of images that has never occurred to me before. The stories I want to tell are different.

It may feel as though another voice is coming through. All of that transformation needs quiet time to do its work. Laurens Van Der Post, in *A Testament to Wilderness*, wrote, "There are no shortcuts in creation. Things happen by the planting and the sowing of seeds, and do not appear all at once. We must have the humility of spirit to recognize how small, in a sense, is the success we can achieve in a single lifetime."

During the silent times, the soul is engaged. It knows this is a time of immersion in awareness, in observation, in the company of the hidden. The ego feels left out; it wants action and products for its identity. We're greedy and want as much of the good stuff as we can get. But it simply doesn't work that way with a creative process that is grounded in the spiritual. You may not write twenty-five books in your lifetime. You may write some fine poems, though. Even if what you do with your writing is to produce a series of journals where your truth is told, what would be wrong with that? If you rush your way through, your impatience will show in the work, and you'll probably not write well. If you push the process, you close off the soul, as sodden as it is with love for stories. The soul of imagination won't be whipped into control.

It's not that you have to wait for divine inspiration. I don't write very often if I wait for that signal. Writing is also an act of will. One that requires determination, intention, and commitment to the work. What's important is to distinguish between laziness, fear, and the fallow periods. The way to know the difference is through experience. If your will can engage your imagination and you write, the inspiration catching on as you go, then write! It may appear to be a subtle difference at first, but as you go you'll be able to distinguish between pushing against your creative self, getting nowhere, and moving into it.

Surviving Wordlessness

When my teaching schedule is full or overfull, I can't write. The teaching comes from a place within that's too similar to writing, and the supply of juice isn't infinite. I spend the creativity in the classroom. At those times, the longing may be there but it's abstract and distant.

My friend Sharman suffers from a chronic illness. She's frequently too exhausted to write. But she longs for it. I've seen the journal and pen on her bedstand, even when she's been in the hospital, critically ill. Most of the hours in her day are taken up with rehabilitation—physical therapy, respiratory therapy. Then it's time to pick her son up from school, prepare dinner—what's left for writing is only the longing.

The novelist Carolyn Chute said:

> *I can't just switch from* life *mode to* writer *mode.* Usually it takes three days to get into the *writer* mode. Three days of quiet non-*life* mode, lots of coffee and no interruptions . . .

> Writing is like meditation . . . or prayer. . . . You are tapping
> into your unconscious. . . . With life banging and popping and
> cuckooing all around, you are not going to find your way to your
> subconscious, which is a place of complete submission.

Many of us simply don't have three days that we can use as transition time to move from "life mode" to "writer mode." We may stay in a state of longing for writing because we don't have the luxury of that amount of time to move toward our writer-selves. Of course, not everyone needs that kind of time. The point is that any number of things can keep us from writing and in a perpetual state of longing until the nudge of that poem fades, and we need time to enter our writer mode.

Rather than abandon the poem or story, how can you acknowledge your longing for deep expression and meet it in a way that fits into your life? The first place to start is always right where you are. Begin by realizing you're away from your creative work for whatever reason. If you're deep into longing, just get out a sheet of paper and write that. Personify it if you like. What color or shape is the longing? How big? You'll find that personification can take the invisible longing and give it symbolic form, which separates it from you so you can see it as a part of who you are, not the whole you.

Alternatively, when you feel as though you've endured a period of not writing long enough and have held yourself in that quietude and inherited its riches, a way to begin writing again is one I learned from William Stafford. Though I never had the chance to study with him personally, I've heard him tell this story to an audience. It's the take-what-comes, don't-be-choosy method. When Stafford's children were young, he used to get up very early in the mornings and go downstairs where he'd make himself toast and instant coffee. He'd take his breakfast to the living room couch, open the curtains, lie back against the pillows, and watch the day begin. Opening his notebook, he would write, taking whatever words came and not being too picky. Apparently his young daughter must have heard him rustling around, so she too began to rise early and go downstairs to be with her dad. Instead of sending her back to bed, Stafford started getting up even earlier, so he could write before going off to teach and also spend time with his sleepy daughter when she came to join him.

The take-what-comes method means you do just that. Whatever words enter your mind, write those down. They sound silly, you think? That's all right. What's next? Engage the curious poet within you who accepts the ridiculous and the sublime equally, who doesn't play favorites to your heftier thoughts. Use your senses. What do you see and hear and smell? Is there a taste to the morning air? What's the texture of darkness fading? Just give your words to the paper, trusting there are more where those came from. Stafford wrote a lot of poems beginning that way. They're nearly conversational, as though I stepped into a chat in progress. And then, by the time I'm nearing the last line of the poem, it's taken me where I didn't expect to go.

During periods of not writing, I'll often pull out my crayons and pastels. I find another form through which to speak that doesn't have the fine edges that words do, that is pure image and color. I'll color with my eyes closed for how the crayon feels in my hand. The glide of purple or the scratch of red unlocks the place where I'm closed to words. It's not that by coloring I'm suddenly inclined to write, it's that the coloring allows the tightness inside me to fall away. Try it. You can use crayons, colored pencils, or whatever appeals to you. Don't worry about drawing something recognizable—go with whatever your hand creates.

For the Notebook 1

What Do You Long to Say?

If you were to truly say what you most long to, what would that be? You may not be able to identify it from the outside, but you can uncover it through writing. Start with one thing you long for, even a seemingly insignificant thing. Write it down and witness it. Don't question it from the outside: no interrogation! Can you step inside that longing and look around? Take the next word and give it to the page. Follow this method and notice how you move from word to word, then from phrase to sentence, and so on. The idea here isn't to make something; it's to be with yourself and with what you long for. Spend a half hour to an hour at your desk in the presence of longing. If you're writing freely, you'll probably end up with several pages of material. This isn't a writing exercise where the goal is a finished paragraph or poem. The goal is the experience of being with the longing and letting it have its say.

For the Notebook 2

LONGING AND THE BODY

Your longing may have taken up house in a part of your body. Where is it? Ask your body where the ache lives. It may move from one place to another. You may feel it in your hands, the pit of your stomach. Mine often settles in my throat, stuck between heart and mouth. Other times I feel it like bricks against my chest, as though they're being held there. It's like an invisible wall separates me from my heart and once I sit with it I discover where it's lodged itself this time. It helps me to stop batting at it like an annoying mosquito. I'll grab my box of colored pencils and a sheet of black paper to etch some color into the darkness of what I am without. Then it shifts. I invite the presence of God in; it shifts again. Just like seeing a lonely friend, I feel great relief in having met it where it lives.

This exercise may not produce a single word. Fifteen minutes may be as much time as you care to spend. Can you give yourself a few moments longer to honor what you are without and to see where within you it exists?

For the Notebook 3

During Wordless Times

One way to be with your writing during the fallow times is to write an accompaniment to the void, to write in your notebook about what the time is like. Is your fallow time a tunnel, a yelling voice, the space of air a wave makes as it curls over? Talk to the wordlessness; ask it what's going on. Then write down what you hear, not with the idea of writing a song or story about it, but with the intention of listening and paying attention, honoring your barrenness.

This is not an exercise to speed up the nonwriting periods, but to help them feel less arid and bleak. I use it often during my wordless times. I like the companionship. Some days five minutes is all I can give. Other days I can write into the longing for half an hour. Again, the integrity of experience is what you're after. No stopwatch allowed here, no particular number of pages required to get an "A" in longing. The more you write, the more you'll notice how the writing will tell you when enough is enough.

CHAPTER 9

QUESTING FOR WORDS AT THE ALTAR OF UNCERTAINTY

One must have chaos in one, to give birth to a dancing star.
Friedrich Nietzsche

Working out of your own discovery, out of your own realization, who's going to want it? Well, you may be surprised. It's a very difficult decision to make, to do this thing that is an experiment, the creating, bringing forth of a form that was never brought forth before.
Joseph Campbell

Her first steps, though cautious, began immediately to reinforce her faith in greater possibilities.
George MacDonald

Chaos in the writing process can feel like meteor showers coming down at you from every direction. The lights are startling and beautiful, but it's all too much and you want to look away, to bury your face in your hands. Or it may feel more like pots and pans crashing out of the cupboard doors and onto the floor. Maybe for you, it's like the 1989 Loma Prieta earthquake when the ground really did open up.

Chaos is not about emptiness, it's about overflow. Something's trying to enter your consciousness and get written down. But in the overflow you feel unable to determine what to write; there's a sense of uncertainty. There are so many words coming forward, they overwhelm you. You're not sure which words will take you to the story you most need to write. Following one idea doesn't feel quite right, but you're not sure following another will be any more certain. You feel lost, lost in the self but nearly out of it, unsure which way to go. A great deal of knowing can come from not knowing, but you've got to hang in the unknown and wait it out. You may be breaking out of the order of the known into new awareness. Chaos will bring forward what's previously been hidden. But you may need to slow the process down and give up trying to get anywhere fast. Today may be a writing day where you just survey the area, notice how many possibilities for your words there are. What made sense yesterday just doesn't hold water today.

Chaos can often come at the beginning of a writing project, just as you're being initiated into it. In *Crossing to Avalon*, Jean Shinoda Bolen writes, "To be initiated into a mystery psychologically is to have a mystical experience that changes you. You no longer are who you were before. You have undergone something that sets you apart from those who have not had the experience. Often an initiation involves an element of isolation, or facing fear or undergoing an ordeal. But perhaps just as often, the initiatory experience comes as a gift of grace, when mystery and profound beauty come together in a numinous moment of which we are a part. . . ." I think of that as the moment the way through becomes apparent and the writing snaps, sizzles, and steams.

SENSES OF DIRECTION

I have a faulty sense of direction. But give me an American city and eventually, after a few twists and turns, I can probably find a fairly decent place for dinner that won't put me over my budget and catch a taxi back to my hotel. I've wandered for hours through Atlanta and D.C., and Seattle I discovered by bicycle. North? South? I couldn't tell you. An inkling of where the road might lead me was lacking, as was the certainty I'd been in that exact spot the day before. Rather quickly, I'm lost.

Having been lost in many places, the ensuing sense of panic and disorientation is not unfamiliar. The sensations are similar to those I experience when lost in writing. It's not casual. As a woman, being lost makes me feel like prey. Being lost in New York City when I was seventeen and being followed by a group of young men who taunted me was scary, but not as frightening as being lost walking in the California hills toward nightfall. At least in New York what I feared was out in the open, and I had some degree of confidence that other people weren't too far away. But in the backcountry, I was afraid of what was hidden from view, what might jump out at me. I was afraid my sense of direction had failed me, that I was all turned around and nowhere seemed to go on forever in all directions. Both times I felt I had to go forward, didn't think that going back would get me found. I kept reminding myself to trust in the walking, that I would find my way by following the walking, the trail or sidewalk, and my vague sense of direction. In writing sometimes I have to walk back to my very first sentence and wind my way through the words, through those thickets and trees, past hope of finding an ending to my poem. When I was lost in the physical world, I succumbed to not knowing just where I was and, to some degree, embraced that. Both times I found my way back to where I wanted to be.

Early last June, Michael and I visited Città di Castello, a small Italian medieval city where one ruddy stone building much resembled the next and the circuitous streets were a maze designed to confuse the uninitiated. We were the uninitiated. Our barely existent grasp of the language would not help us find our way. My innate strategy when exploring a new place, in order to prevent the possibility of getting lost, is boring and always the same: venture a few blocks in one direction, turn around and walk back to where I started, try a few blocks in another direction, note what's where, turn around, then go inside for tea. It's like putting a toe in the lake to see just how cold the water is. Eventually the swimmer gets completely wet, but it takes a while. Michael has a different approach. A few hours after settling into the apartment with the tiny rose garden, we began walking. And walking. I protested, "We don't know where we are." "I know," he said, continuing on, turning left here, right there. A few blocks later I asked, "OK, do you know how to get back?" Unfazed, he said, "No." But he didn't stop and turn around or even look back over his shoulder. He kept walking. So I did too.

Obviously, there are issues of gender at work here, a tradition that the man goes out to explore the world, becomes the hero, the conqueror. But what was most interesting to me that first evening in Italy was the awareness that getting lost and recognizing that you are lost is the first step to finding your way, and how this pertains to writing and spiritual seeking.

BEING LOST IN LANGUAGE

In the midst of writing you may feel you have entered an unknown that more resembles what you consider a nonplace—marked by haze and shrouded forms—than a destination. When we are lost in writing, we are at once nowhere and everywhere. But there aren't really any nowheres, just many places we haven't been before. We aren't sure which words are the next right ones to put down on the paper. Or the words have not led us where we thought they would. It's unsettling. We may feel we have no foothold and are floundering. In the process of floundering, we may stumble upon a direction that would never have occurred to us otherwise. When we're desperate we become more willing to accept what we wouldn't if we felt secure and certain, and that can bring us to the unexpected, the amazing, and the mysterious.

Your foot finds a tree root that's stable, and you hold on to the side of the mountain, catching your breath, cursing all the while. But wait, look at the view from this precarious spot—billows of fog rushing in toward the mountain.

Being directionless and uncertain is part of both writing and the spiritual process—and necessary. Not pleasant, but necessary. These emotions can invigorate our faith like nothing else, help us to rediscover what it's founded on. In the gospels, Christ said, "He who would save his life must lose it." Faith is one way we take leaps in our writing and make new discoveries. When we're in a new place and don't know exactly where we are, we do begin to find our way.

To be lost in the writing process is different from experiencing writer's block. At those times, we experience not only a loss of direction, but an absence of language, a sense of being cut off from words and the home place they issue from. When we're lost, there may be lots of language, but we're not sure where it's taking us, which is confusing. Internal chaos is like many electrical charges misfiring at once. Your head feels dark and big inside. It's a mild, momentary madness.

Confusion allows us to approach language and spiritual practice from a new vantage point. The language comes differently; it may be more jumbly, more frenetic, and less typical of how we usually write. Being lost we encounter the power of the sublime. We may forge a vision out of what doesn't work. And as the writer Susan Griffin said, "The more I trusted myself, the closer I came to the vision." Trust yourself to find the vision and then to believe in it.

When physically lost, we notice the details of our location in an effort to distinguish the familiar from what is foreign, to help us find our way. When we're lost to the words' direction, to the pull of spirit, we again look to find what we recognize in an effort to know where we are, who we are. There's a lot that comes toward the surface when we're scrambling to find our way. When we've moved out of the limits of the predictable into what is surprising and new, we are more available to mystery. When we are in unfamiliar surroundings we have the opportunity to experience things in an original way that is further from ready association. It's a stretch. We compare what is new, that which we may distrust, with what we know and trust. We become alert and attentive to nuances and details—textures, the weather, noises—which might otherwise go unnoticed. We have the opportunity to see the layers of shadow and the variations of light.

It's like this: you're writing away and everything is moving along just fine. Your pencil's sharp, the words a dime a dozen, and those available are just the ones you can use. The form of the piece is taking shape. You've got a sense of the beginning, an inkling toward the middle, and faith that the end will be there waiting when you come for it. But suddenly, for no outward reason, the direction is lost and you're unsure which way to go. You try clearing your throat but the tightness only intensifies. It's like you believed in something but don't anymore, a fall from grace. For some writers, actual physical sensations accompany this state of being. My throat feels constricted and my chest feels like a door slammed shut on it. When you're looking for what feels like the answer and can't find it, it's frustrating. Sometimes this frustration borders on anxiety and the physical sensations are a result of that. It can take a great effort to stay present and focused but that's what's most helpful—not to worry about whether the work is becoming itself but to be an explorer and see where the writing may take you. Rainer Maria Rilke described it this way, "I feel close to what language can't reach." So there you are trying through language to reach what may feel beyond it, or nearly. And still, as a writer on the journey, the desire is to get as close as you can.

WRITING AS A SPIRITUAL QUEST

If you were to consider your writing life as a kind of spiritual quest, perhaps that would make the moments of feeling lost along the way more tolerable. Robert Torrance, in his book *The Spiritual Quest*, says, "If the spiritual quest is a fundamental human activity rooted in biology, psychology, and language, it will find expression throughout the world and throughout the ages in the supremely important acts and stories embodied in religious rituals and myths." So you're part of a long-standing tradition that's been a part of many cultures for eons.

You may be solitary in creating the material of your quest, its particular direction, but you're one of many in whom the desire to seek is an active spiritual motivation. Torrance goes on to say, "The widely variant cultural refractions of the quest are essential properties of a creatively self-transformative process. . . ." Transformation occurs over time. Creativity is fed by the quest.

To choose writing as the form the quest takes is to make a scaffold upon which to place and experience your journey. The goal of a spiritual quest is to transform the limitations of your universe. That's no small thing. To attempt a quest is to begin a journey that will take you up close and personal to your own limits. It requires a spirit of adventure and a bit of bravery. If you want to write your soul, why would that call for anything less than the risk of getting lost? Maxine Hong Kingston talks about it this way, "I do feel we are on that quest. . . . I pictured the hero as the artist, the artist going on explorations, and how it is very possible to lose your way. . . ." Exploration in writing keeps the writing new and unprepared for. That's living!

Difficulty is implied by the idea of a quest. What you meet along the way may not be what you bargained for. But there in front of you is a pack of wolves, so what are you going to do? The way through may not be the most obvious one. If you can't divert the wolves' attention by throwing a large rock a few feet away (because you don't have such a rock), maybe you can tilt your head back, join in their howling, and they'll relax a bit in your presence. Or maybe you can slink quietly away. The terrain you've got to tread may not suit you. You'll need your own resourcefulness to survive. Barging on ahead is the American way. But it's not your soul's way. The soul is known moment by moment, not just in the final destination.

All this holds us to the quest, keeps us yearning and attempting, looking for a way. Joseph Campbell put it perfectly, "It's not the *agony* of the quest, but the *rapture* of the revelation." There is agony in a quest but it's superceded later by the rapture when you feel like Emily Dickinson who said, "If I feel physically as if the top of my head were taken off, I know that is poetry. . . . Is there any other way to know?" When the writing finds its path again and I'm on it, I get that feeling like after a bout with a bad flu; I'm lightheaded and elated. My heart skips, as do my feet if I let them.

Campbell also says, "A hero ventures forth from the world of common day into a region of supernatural wonder. . . ." To take on a spiritual writing quest, you'll see how with just a pen and paper you too can move beyond the common into the supernatural. When a writer is questing the whole day actually appears different. It unfolds word by word and the colors are brighter, the sounds more precise. The journey will take you to more beauty than you may expect. There's something magical about arriving at the sublime and beautiful that comes from yourself. It's surprising to me, for one thing. And though I may be one small person doing her life's work as she sees fit, there are times through writing when the words truly leap off the paper. And that wouldn't have happened if I didn't keep my trousers to the chair and my fingers on the keys.

The Writer's Journey

You may embark on a quest inspired to follow a vision. Each time you sit down to write it's a kind of miniquest. You have a vision, even an oblique one, of what you want to say. You feel pulled to speak, drawn toward words you can't anticipate. You're striving to get to what's beyond the bend. Leaving the rational, daily world behind, you enter the realm of imagination and soul, which is akin to dream life, where the rules are different from those of ordinary life and the view is not the same as the one from your bedroom window. Through writing, if you're lucky, you meet the vision and transform it into story. To join your vision through writing is to fully embrace it, to find the language for it and bring it home. Campbell said, "The Hero is the one who has gone on the adventure and brought back the message." The story or poem is the message the writer returns with from the journey.

In the broader sense of writing as a quest, the writer's entire life is a journey toward the heart of language and where it will lead. You're being pulled not just toward one story but toward a life of stories. You can't know what you'll find there or what you'll be called to say. You only know that through writing you discover what you need to say. This is often a difficult thing to have faith in, because you must rely heavily on the unknown, what's yet to come. There are no promises of external success.

You can quest for language your whole life and nothing is guaranteed. But if you're on a quest, you have to keep going. There's no turning back. You can't unwrite your words. But one word does follow the one before and so on until there's a phrase, a sentence, then a paragraph, and so on into life's chapters. There's a life of words and their meaning. When questing for language, that's the call you're responding to.

The Long Way Around

At the beginning of *The Divine Comedy,* Dante writes, "Midway on our life's journey, I found myself / In dark woods, the right road lost." He looks up and in the distance sees the sun rising, his goal in sight. His desire for the light is palpable. Dante tries to reach the light directly and almost immediately encounters three beasts—a leopard, a lion, and a she-wolf—that will not let him pass. They force him back down into the darkness, where he is met by the soul of Virgil who explains that the only way to get to the light is to take the long way around; there is no shortcut. Dante has to go back and risk the frightening descent into hell and then make the difficult ascent through purgatory.

The poet John Ciardi writes, "The point of the parable is that in art as in theology—as in all things that concern people in their profoundest moments—the long way round is the only way home. One who seeks mortal understanding must go the long way." To take the long way around in writing and in spiritual practice, the only place you can start is where you are, no matter how you feel about that place. It means stepping in, attending to each thing—each image, thought, feeling, and inclination—as it appears and, by attending to it, bring it to the light. You can't rush the experience even if you'd like to take the straight, quick path back to the light.

To move past the chaos on your journey, pick up a pen and write about what you have lost yourself in; do this till you find your way again. Bring yourself back to the path. At times, you may have to let go of your initial writing plans and subject temporarily, look at where you truly are lost, and literally put that down. Write the words for what it's like to be lost in the writing process, however absurd they sound as they hit the paper. According to the playwright David Mamet, "When you sit down to write, tell the truth from one moment to the next and see where it takes you." Your truth will change; it's not set in cement, but rather has fluidity.

Sometimes chaos overwhelms us when we don't recognize that our truth has changed and when we try to follow a predetermined intention which, for whatever reason, no longer fits. At these times, as writer Sallie Tisdale claims, "You don't write. You get out of the way." You don't have to invest in the chaos; pull up a chair but don't build a monument to it. Just let it be and be ready for it to move aside as new language comes and you continue on your quest.

LANGUAGE AS A MIRROR TO THE WORLD

Rainer Maria Rilke, in a letter to the painter Paul Cézanne, wrote, "Surely all art is the result of one's having been in danger of having gone through an experience all the way to the end, to where no one can go any further." I know that's true for me, that often the impulse to write comes out of having felt and thought my way through an experience as far as I could, and then the next thing was to write about it. Writing can be a way to process and heal from an experience. It helps integrate the experience in a way that nothing else will. Talking it to a friend or therapist won't get me there, nor will a bike ride. I have to write my way into the experience in order to know it fully, to know its potential teaching. Through writing I'm found again. It's another side of being lost. You can be lost in writing, and you can be lost in life and found through writing. What do you want your language to do? How will it be a mirror of the life you are trying to live?

Author Andre Dubus wrote, "Making sandwiches while sitting in a wheelchair is not physically difficult. But it can be a spiritual trial; the chair always makes me remember my legs, and how I lived with them. . . . The memory of having legs that held me upright at this counter and the image of simply turning from the counter and stepping to the drawer are the demons I must keep at bay, or I will rage and grieve because of space, and time, and this wheeled thing that has replaced my legs. So I must try to know the spiritual essence of what I am doing." What is the spiritual essence of what you're doing with writing? Answers to that question fuel the quest. Are you uncovering your past or working to unite language with spirit? Are you driven to tell just one story but to tell it so nothing's left out? Do you want your words to describe something you saw for a fraction of an instant but want to see again, this time in words of your own making? How to make language transcend itself is big work. For it to go beyond mere sound and shapes on paper requires devotion.

Writing can be a difficult master. To be willing to venture into the life of the writer you've got to be hungry, really hungry for words because the way is not necessarily smooth and easy. Words won't always come at your calling. They won't always shape into what you want them to. There are dead ends and wild-goose chases. There are days when the blank page stares back at you all day long because nothing seems right. For many of us the desire to be with language and where it comes from and to work with the words overrides the obstacles. But not every day. Some days you may want to just sit on the side of the path and witness your process. Or you may weep yourself to sleep at night having not found one good word for days.

Keeping the metaphor of quest in mind may be helpful. You can remind yourself that just like a physical journey in the wilderness your writing quest has landslides and groundswells. I find it helps to see what I'm doing on a continuum, by remembering that this isn't just one day of writing and its accompanying trials; it's a whole life through language. Writing is my walking stick. It helps me have the faith and tenacity, and at times the courage, to go where I'm called.

PREPARING FOR THE JOURNEY

When initiating the writer's quest you should move with practice, skill, and intuition. None of them alone will take you as far as they will together. The journey requires you to be prepared for what you cannot entirely be prepared for. You have to be ready for the unknown to appear, for a fit of words that seems to come from nowhere and tells you all you didn't want to know. Acceptance of this will open your heart. With an open heart all you have to say will come pouring through. An imperative of the quest is that the seeker trust the authority of his own experience. You're out here alone and can't rely on anyone else's judgment, not in your initial writing drafts, anyway.

Before beginning any journey, decide what you'll bring with you, what you'll need for various kinds of weather. There are those of us who will also think about what to wear. My hiking boots are right for one kind of journey, my black Italian sandals with the square heel for another. When the author Iris Origo was fleeing from her home in Italy that was being taken over by the Germans during World War II, she had time to grab just a few things and amid her essentials, thought to stash a bottle of eau de cologne in her bag.

Even metaphorical journeys require survival kits. So, as you prepare for your quest into the world of writing, what will you bring? For my journey, I carry my friend Marion's voice telling me in her patient way, "Hard doesn't mean bad." That's all she has to say and I can fill in the rest. It means that even when the writing gets difficult, even when I've temporarily lost my way in it, that's not an indication that I should turn away from the work. A thermos of Barry's Irish tea with plenty of cream and sugar both soothes and invigorates. I bring gloves to keep my hands warm for writing in the cold, which I do sometimes when it's winter and I need to breathe the salty ocean air.

If you consider the points of view you want to be open to, the landscapes you want to translate into words, the people who will inhabit your stories, you might consider bringing them along. Chances are they'll come anyway. Bring a metaphor or physical symbol for whatever it is you're reaching for in your work. At one spot along the Pacific coast, no matter when I go there, the hard sand is littered with smooth rocks no bigger than dimes. I look at them as steps along the path I'm making here in my study with words. A few of the stones that I've pocketed upon occasion sit on the shelf above my desk. I need lots of metaphors in my life—images to suck on like lozenges. I need reminders of who I am and where I'm going.

Other things will want to come with you, like the neighbor cat who tries to sneak into the car. As valuable as it is to choose what to bring, it may be as or more important to think about what you wish to leave behind, far behind, under lock and key. It may take years to realize what you've been carrying blindly, and more time to actually dump it out of the bag.

We've talked about the internal critic, that loud "No, no, no, you can't do it" voice. I practice leaving that voice behind over and over. But it's sneaky and old, and no sooner do I get into a good writing pace, than I may notice it's come along after all and I have to contend with it yet again. But nearly a year into writing this book, the critic's not as noisy and insistent. My soul knows what it's doing and does it almost every day. If I remember to rest, eat right, say my prayers, and exercise, the critic seems to have trust in me or in something that I don't want to mess with by talking about too much!

My calendar is another thing I don't want to take on my daily writing journey but have a hard time leaving behind. It only tells me what's outside and away from now—where I have to be later, what I'll have to do when, and who I'll need to be at that time. It's also not a good idea to carry your phonebook because there are all kinds of people you could call, but then the writing day would be diminished and inappropriately inhabited by someone else's story that may not belong in what you're writing.

Before you begin the next phase of your writing quest consider what you want to take along and what you need to leave behind. But don't stop there; be diligent about revisiting your needs. Consider the spirit of the writer within and what you need for the words to be written. If you're anything like me, you'll need to reconsider this over and over again.

The Map

The scientist and writer Alfred Korzybski said, "The map is not the territory." Now say that to yourself twenty times. The map isn't the territory. It won't tell you about weather conditions or how you'll feel along the way. If it's a quest you're on, there is no map for your specific journey, though guides have been created by others after the fact which may assist you on your way. I hope this book serves as a map for you. What I consider difficult may be a breeze for you. At least a map can provide you with something to respond to or break away from. My backpacking husband frequently leaves the trail behind and cross-countries his way up the mountainside. I wouldn't dare doing that if I were without him on a trail. But with pencil and paper I keep making maps and then finding they tell the way to somewhere I once wanted to go but not where I'm headed any longer. So I erase or scratch out that part and diagram it again—where I think I'm going, anyway. The writer Wendy Battin said, "I know my map is provisional, that I have pieced it together out of my own need. . . ." The map comes out of our innate need to find our way, to be able to look ahead and do more than put one foot in front of the other. It comes out of the human need for support and guidance and knowledge, that, "Yes, as much as this journey is my own, others have also taken it."

Who Will Accompany Me?

The act of writing itself is solitary. You're alone in your room with paper and pen and all that goes on in your mind and soul. But when I'm lost, I want to invite another into my room, for a friend to join me for awhile in my writing life. Then I call for help, abashedly at times, desperate and unashamed at others. Sometimes I need a reader to help me pick and sort, gather and discard, name signposts along the way for what they are. I've had more than one poem that I worked and worked at alone and then shared with another writer; having another take on the piece aided me in seeing what was present and what wasn't, what worked and what didn't. I E-mailed a piece I was struggling with to my friend Sharman. She didn't solve the problem for me, but she gave me an outsider's words for what she saw in the poem and that helped me to see it more clearly. That poem is still unfinished and maybe will never become itself. But maybe it has led me to poems that wouldn't have come if it hadn't been attempted first.

Other times I need a companion in being lost. Over the phone a close friend will say, "You're lost all right. You won't be there forever." The exact words don't matter much. What does matter is to be seen just where I am. Really, it's only through getting lost in the process that we find the whole story. But we need to be reminded of this at times, to be accompanied in this knowledge, to not feel alone. When choosing whom to ask for companionship when you're lost, consider other writer friends, those whose opinions you trust. The advantage of talking to other writers is that, for one thing, they write and are familiar with that world, and for another, they know about being lost in language. But what matters most is to seek out someone who loves you and who is supportive of your writing.

A LITTLE DIVERSION

Just as when the critic's in the room and I can't find the poet within, when I am lost to my words' direction and feel sunk in the despair of it, a diversion may be called for. I'll go to the garage, grab the broom, walk into the living room, and look for the sagging lines of cobwebs that straggle from picture frame to lamp shade to mantle to room corner to windowsill in strings of decoration that for months may go unnoticed. Down come the webs. The dust-covered, sticky fiber wraps around the broom. Once the room is clear, I go back to my desk hoping the same has occurred in my mind.

At times, while attending to mundane activities, my confusion will lift enough to find a sentence that seems to take me in a direction that interests me and is authentic. It's a relief to have removed myself from my work for a few moments. When I go back I'm at a little distance from it and not under so much pressure.

RESPONDING TO UNCERTAINTY IN YOUR WRITING

You might reread your piece slowly, going through it bit by bit and paying attention to when you first feel confused. At that moment stop and ask yourself, "What's missing here, what am I unsure of?" In her book *Never Eat Your Heart Out*, Judith Moore comments, "When writing's not going well, it's true that you do well to look for what's missing." Ask, "What am I feeling, thinking, tuning out?" Wait for the answer, don't push ahead. You may find you need to cut something out, that it doesn't belong there; it's another story. You may find you need to write further into the confusion and find your answer there. Now you have to become not only a writer but a reader. The most important point I can stress is that this process takes time. Confusion doesn't clear on demand. To berate yourself for being without the answer sets you back and is limiting. That kind of criticism helps no one.

INTO THE MARVELOUS

What I sometimes know in writing, but have a more difficult time trusting in new places, is that when I'm not intent on remaining in the familiar, when I'm willing to venture, I end up in some pretty cool places. That first night of wandering blindly in Città di Castello, Michael and I found ourselves before a large building with mosaics on the outer walls. It looked as if the pale, translucent tiles had been made from bits of shell, the way they caught the light cast from a street lamp. Walking further we found an old stone tower.

In C. S. Lewis's *The Lion, the Witch and the Wardrobe*, Lucy, the young protagonist, explores an old house and looks into a closet filled with many coats ("There was nothing Lucy liked so much as the smell and feel of fur"). She goes deeper into the closet, finding a second row of coats in the darkness. She suddenly realizes there is "something crunching under her feet, something hard and rough and even prickly" like the branches of trees against her hands. And then she knows she is not in a wardrobe at all. Lucy is no longer where she once was.

Lucy entered a place she'd probably never even imagined. She walked from the known, through the closet of coats, to the marvelous. She could have gotten there no other way than, as Michael and I did, venturing forth. You don't always make the jump from the known to the marvelous without first being in the thick of confusion. It's like you have to surrender to the possibility of your own failure and touch the resistance to unknowing first. Author E. L. Doctorow says, "You have to surrender to the act of writing, give up to it, and trust that if you have anything, it will discover it for you." The writing will discover you and come forward through the whirlwind of not knowing where to go. The writing will move into those coats and part them.

The move from chaos to clarity is gradual. But if you get up from your desk and leave your practice for the day in the tumult of confusion, you might miss that moment. Then, in memory, the writing time will hold only the ache of disappointment and a feeling of wanting, the knowledge that you abandoned something that may have been possible. You'll have deprived yourself of the struggle.

What if confusion wasn't something to get out of as quickly as possible? What might be found there? Confusion offers us a time to drop into our own complex multifacetedness, to be in that abundance.

Remember there's more at play than meets the eye or the brain or the heart. There's a larger integrity behind you. The veracity and intactness of the work lie beyond the chaos. Even when you can't touch them, they're present. At least consider the possibility that what you're at work on, even when you're twisted by confusion over it, is whole and complete.

WANDERING BACK

Back to that evening in Italy. Michael and I found our way back to our garden apartment quite late in the evening, having taken a rather circuitous route around many tight corners, the buildings right up against the road, where inside and above life was going on, quiet conversations, lights turning off for the night. Though we stood right in front of our apartment building I hadn't any inkling of where we were. Patient and loving man that he is, Michael took my hand and we stooped to enter the low courtyard door, struggled to get the key to turn in the lock for the first time, and put ourselves to bed. What had we found on our quest? The engraved, illuminated outer walls of the *pinacoteca*, the duomo with its wide steps, and the *gelateria* we would return to on subsequent evenings. I'd also found that wandering had brought us back to where we wanted to be. So long as we remained on the mazelike streets within the walled city we couldn't really get lost, though for moments we were certainly unfound.

For the Notebook 1

BUILDING AN ALTAR OF UNCERTAINTY

Imagine an actual altar of uncertainty, a physical place that represents the complexity of your chaos. An altar is a place of reverence where holy objects sit. You may find it hard to consider your uncertainty holy, but it is the key to your greatest knowing. To concretize the abstract makes it more tangible; giving it form takes some of the onus off it. If you picture uncertainty as an actual thing, you can work with it, bring it from obscurity into view. You might even draw a picture of it.

Students I've worked with on this have imagined all kinds of places that represent their uncertainty. Recently, at a workshop in San Jose, one woman's packed altar contained, among many other things, ransom notes. So there's a price for uncertainty. What's in danger if uncertainty is ignored? Another woman imagined a wide slab of granite. Finally she rested her cheek on its cool surface and felt relief, instead of continuing to turn away from it and toward only what she knew, the predictable.

What shape does your altar have? How tall does it stand? Are its edges rounded or square? At what distance is it from your desk? Is it behind or in front of you? What sits on it? Do sounds come from those things? What do they mean to you and how did they get there? You might draw a picture of the altar. What prayers do you say there? And who listens to them?

My altar is taller than I am and narrow, stands about five feet eight inches. It's a precarious structure with thin, spindly legs of different lengths. Its top is tilted and is as slippery as though it had been greased. The objects there are discomforting—my mother's false teeth, the box of a stranger's ashes, dirty water in a glass. There's a circa 1950s patent leather purse with a cheap snap-clasp: all my confused pieces gather dust there. The collection of objects continually slides toward the edge. I always try to get there at the right time to catch them before anything slips off. Whatever's there risks transformation, becoming unsightly, blemished, or rancid. At least that is my fear. Caught praying here, my knees bleed. I can no longer stand up straight. I pray for ugly things, have no determination, have abandoned faith.

But if I stay prostrate long enough, humbling myself before the unknown that burdens me, the transformation is of another kind. I am no longer running from what I do not understand, from what feels larger than my physical body. Rather I am present, and through that arrive at a place of momentary freedom, relieved of the weight of not knowing. It's not that I'm suddenly moved into great confidence and certainty, but having an acceptance of my own chaos and making a place for it calms me down.

You might make an actual writing altar in a corner of your room or out in the garden, or a temporary altar could be erected at the beach. Draw a picture of such a place, or write it into being in your notebook. Give yourself a little time for this one, an hour or so, with no one pulling you in another direction.

For the Notebook 2

JUST WHAT HAVE YOU LOST?

A few years ago I began thinking of all the things I'd ever lost, had stolen, or through poor judgment had sold or given away. It wasn't just the red ten-speed I'd lent to a lousy boyfriend that got stolen from his garage and for which he never paid me a dime, but the bigger things like my faith in God, my virginity. When you lose something, you also find something, but it's often not the thing you thought would be there. You lose a friend and find loneliness. You lose a piece of the past and invent another to take its place. You lose something far away and what you find is near.

What have you lost? Try writing a list of losses, both catastrophic and minute. The ones that have great importance may sit beside the ones you consider nearly irrelevant. Include physical things, dreams, ways of life. Write a list poem; simply catalog everything you've lost in whatever order those losses come down the pike of your imagination. Then consider the order, based on not only meaning, but sound. You might try a few versions of this poem. Spend twenty minutes writing your list and plan on another twenty or so for revising its order and making it whole. Or write into one experience of loss. If you've ever lost your faith, what have you found in its place and what was it like when the faith returned? Or is it still out there somewhere wandering among the dead?

CHAPTER 10

TWIG, STONE, SKY

Sacred Places, Silence, and Solitude

God grows everywhere, like grass.
Kelly Cherry, from Natural Theology

We believe that all living things are spiritual beings. Spirits
can be expressed as energy forms manifested in matter. . . .
A blade of grass is an energy form manifested in matter . . .
grass matter. The spirit of the grass is that unseen
force which produces the species of grass, and
it is manifest to us in the form of real grass.

The Mohawk People

At a certain point you say to the woods, to the sea, to the
mountains, the world, now I am ready. Now I
will stop and be wholly attentive.

Annie Dillard

D. H. Lawrence, in his last poems, writes, "To the Etruscan all was alive; the whole universe lived; and the business of man was himself to live amid it all. He had to draw life into himself, out of the wandering huge vitalities of the world. The cosmos was alive, like a vast creature. . . . The whole thing was alive, and had a great soul, or *anima*; and in spite of one great soul, there were myriad roving, lesser souls; every man, every creature and tree and lake and mountain and stream, was animate, and had its own peculiar consciousness." To reclaim this belief in places and beings is to reinvigorate a spiritual awareness of them. We can draw life into our images and words this way. What is the peculiar consciousness of the light on the hillside before dusk? It shimmers a dusty orange hue I've never seen before, despite the fact that I've had more than a few summers looking out this kitchen window just before dinnertime. Something's waking up again.

In their book *Myth of the Goddess: Evolution of an Image*, Anne Baring and Jules Cashford say that to recognize the life in all beings is not an easy thing to do "after centuries of being dismissed as pantheism by orthodox religion, or a childish fantasy by Baconian and Newtonian science and Cartesian philosophy." So, somewhere in the home place within us, where our soul-selves reside, the knowledge of the aliveness of all beings resides as well. Through writing we can once again encounter that belief. We can foster our knowing of place as sacred by writing our way into the places we love, those that we newly encounter, all the places that hold significance for us.

When in nature, we are with that which is larger than ourselves. This is the realm where the unscreened presence of the elements—water, air, earth, fire—are pure, vibrant, visible. In nature we witness mystery. There I'm in the immediate, in the presence of what I don't understand. Human is so small and nature's grand. There I'm away from but also near and inside. A spark of recognition fires within.

One of the most important needs we have is to be rooted, to have a place and feel connected to it. For as much as I may feel at home in the small city where I live, it's in the natural world where I am truly rooted. To be rooted implies permanence, the roots go down. And because they do, because they're secure in the muck and mud of the dark depths, they set a foundation for what is to happen above ground.

Where are you rooted? What is burrowed in among your roots? What things grow there? What white pebbles have lodged themselves between the strands of root fiber? What leaves have fallen down and mulched into the ground, bringing with them hints of light and sky and wind, the movement above ground, the unfetteredness of that?

THIS SOMEWHERE, THIS TREE

Somewhere is better than anywhere.

FLANNERY O'CONNOR

Many years ago I heard the poet Robert Bly give a reading. What most struck me was one thing he said. I can't quote it for you here and I can't say what follows is exactly what he meant, but it's what I've carried with me, my understanding and my awakening. What I understood Bly to say is that there isn't *any* tree, there is only *this* tree or *that* tree, and to remember that when writing a poem. Each tree is itself and, as itself, is unique. I knew that to be true, but I'd never heard it said so clearly and so magically before. The church where the reading was given was dimly lit, the sanctuary dark. Bly was at the front of the room with his out-of-tune bazuki, strumming it now and then, reading Kabir and Rumi, Mirabai, his own work, repeating each poem two times, changing the emphasis. But it was that one thing that riveted me. And every poem that followed his "this tree" statement, I heard in a new way. I listened for the "thisness" in each one. How was the poem *this* God, *this* heart, *this* waterfall? I began to approach my writing in a new way, seeking to see the particular qualities inherent in whatever I was writing. I now bring more sensory awareness to my subjects and greater attention than I had before. That seeing of a thing's uniqueness shows us its spirit. Then we can observe the God within all things. We see what's new and note that; we recognize the familiar and record that.

Look how particularly Toni Morrison, in her novel *Beloved*, describes this place: "There was only one door to the house and to get to it from the back you had to walk all the way around to the front of 124, past the storeroom, past the cold house, the privy, the shed, on around to the porch. And to get to the part of the story she liked best, she had to start way back: hear the birds in the thick woods, the crunch of leaves underfoot; see her mother making her way up into the hills where no houses were likely to be. . . ."

You won't confuse that house with another; her details are specific. She brings readers to the house with her. They're not random details either, the description is representative of the entire book. She invites you not only into the house, but into her story.

How small can you see? What level of detail do you want to bring into your writing? How much spirit and soul? How much breath and blood and bone? If you look out at a summer California field, there's the field. Or there's the grass tilting in the wind. Or light flourishing onto land. Or the sky contrasted against the ground. Or whatever particularities you see, hear, taste, touch, and smell. Joseph Bruchac says, "Every place is the center of the world. Black Elk said that to John Neihart, but almost any medicine person will vouch for its truth."

WITNESSING THE SACRED IN
THE NATURAL WORLD

To witness the sacred in a place, it isn't as though you have to do something grand; you just have to let your eyes do what they were born for and see with the fiber of your self, its muscle and longing. The photographer Walker Evans made the mistake, like most of us do, of trying too hard: "I used to try to figure out precisely what I was seeing all the time until I discovered I didn't need to. If the thing is there, why there it is."

We've got to take our blinders off and slow down if we're to know the world. In witnessing what the sacred places hold, it helps to give the heart of your attention to the details. Is five minutes writing about one blade of grass too long a time or not long enough? Can you spend an hour? How about a week? How does the grass embody spirit? What brings you to knowing it? And how well can we know a piece of grass? A seven-year-old student of mine, Jessica, wrote this poem:

Nothing at All
There is a tree
in the bottom of my heart
with no leaves, no leaves at all.
There is a white tree.
It is white because it is magic.
It is magic because it is snowing.
And beside it is nothing, nothing at all.
Except for a blade of grass, it is all alone.

She doesn't say much about that blade of grass, but she tells us all we need to know. The blade of grass is the tree's companion. The tree is lonely but not entirely. There is magic in the scene too, and no one stays lonely forever when magic's afoot. Jessica didn't need to tell us everything, she needed to choose to tell us *a* something, to bring herself and *her* something into the poem. And she did.

SACRED PLACE AND MEMORY

The rustle of an olive grove has something very secret in it and something very old.

VINCENT VAN GOGH

I discovered sex the first time I walked in the woods. I was in the eighth grade. We kept our clothes on, and our hands didn't wander under the outer layer. His name was Patrick Brady and he introduced me to the natural world in a way that, as a girl who'd only been recently transplanted from New York City to a provincial seaside town, I had never known. Before Pat, nature had been something to stay at a distance from; but that boy made me feel differently about a few things. On one of our first outings, Pat took me to the woods. We walked up the hill from my house to the property of the new university campus that more closely resembled a nature preserve than a college setting. We walked a long way into a forest, past any sign of other people, to a hillside in the dark room of a redwood grove near flowing water. It was winter, drizzly and cold. Sitting there, I smelled nature for the first time. It was the first time I can recall associating a particular smell with the outdoors and knowing it as beautiful; it was the smell of pine. This boy and I sat very close together, holding hands and kissing. He had blond hair and peach fuzz. I liked the smell of him mixed with the smell of the dark forest.

On that afternoon I found out something I hadn't known until then, having never kissed before: when you kiss, you don't just feel it in your mouth. Pat took me places I had never been and we arrived only partway on foot. I felt transported. Holding his hand kept me from going off somewhere distant that I might not return from, and I only half wanted to go. There was something else with us in those woods and, contrary to what I'd thought, it wasn't bugs and it wasn't scary and it wouldn't hurt me. What I felt was the spirit of nature. What surprised me was that I was not separate, but a part of it. Perhaps I was someplace where I belonged.

Whenever I return to that spot in the woods, and I have many times, I feel my body in nature and that I am made of more than flesh and bone. That one spot in the forest where we sat causes a rippling underneath my skin. I discovered more than sex there; I found that there was more in nature than fear could keep me away from. In the natural world I feel tied to something beyond myself that holds my body but does not contain it, that holds my mind but loosens it. Had it not been for Pat Brady, I don't know whether I'd have experienced nature like that. He came into my life at a time when I was needy and open.

Before my outing with Pat, I'd experienced a sense of the sacred in church and at home when alone or through the voice of my mother, but never unbounded like that and never connected so consciously

via my body to another person. Years passed before I ever wrote in a
forest, but the sexual magnetism of the natural world has pulled at me
since. When Pat and I walked out of the woods and back onto the
road, it was as though we crossed a line. The rules were different out
here where everyone's so visible to each other and you have to wait at
the crosswalk for the light to change. The choices felt limited com-
pared to walking pathlessly under trees.

Now there are other places where I have walked in nature that also
hold memory. It's as though the memories themselves are lodged in
tree branches or stuck under rocks for safekeeping. They're sheltered
in the air. It's not only natural places where this has occurred for me,
but the experiences seem less diluted by other events that occur on the
street or indoors, where the bulk of my life is lived and one memory
must cover over the one that came before. The world of sidewalks and
shopping malls is more filled with things, wedded to the familiar. It's
harder for me to find the sacred realm away from nature except in
churches.

Place can hold memory, but we also carry our places invisibly
with us. Joseph Bruchac wrote me that "there are also places that stay
with me, Chief Mountain in Oklahoma where I watched a sunrise
and burned cedar two decades ago, a white sand beach on the coast
of West Africa close to the old slave fort of Elmina, places where the
human spirit in joy and in grief, joined my heart, gave me words,
gave me peace, purpose, the start of a new song." What places stay
with you? How do you embody them? How do they enter into your
writing? Or do they? You might invite them in and see what happens.
Writing makes us pay attention; we have to in order to have something
to say. To give attention to a place changes our perception of it.

BEING AND WRITING IN HOLY PLACES

In *The Sacred Place: Witnessing the Holy in the Physical World*, the editor Scott
Cairns questions whether a sacred place is in tension with the concept
of home. What's sacred about home isn't the same as my experience

of being in what I consider sacred places. But a sense of the sacred is also something I find in my home. It's primarily through writing that I enter what feels like a sacred place and transforms these walls into something beyond the everyday. God can find us anywhere. The sense of stability that I have here, in my home, I know in a way I never have before. That knowing is love, loving and being loved and the grace of that divinity makes room for holiness.

For a place to be recognized as sacred, it must be considered special and have qualities that make it so. Then it is revered and treated with respect, though not necessarily by all who go there. I'm certain that the redwood forest on the college campus that I discovered as sacred may have been a spot for general disregard, wild parties, inattention. In order for us to experience a place as sacred, we need to see the holy in it. Is any place not sacred? Sacred space is beyond ownership. Just as we can't own the sacred, we can't possess that essence that gives a place its holiness. That which makes anything blessed can't be humanly contained.

Joy Harjo writes, "As a poet and writer I am often categorized as a 'place' writer, a Southwestern writer because my writing appears to have been born and has evolved from the fierce scarlet imagination of the land of New Mexico. And it's true, that this place has imagined me, carried me inside its own process of becoming." I love that thought! To be associated with a place, to be imagined and remembered by it. And how true; I would not be who I am if I had grown up and lived elsewhere. Manhattan's early morning sounds are way in the back of me. I breathe them in still.

Naomi Shihab Nye says, "[Robert] Bly talks about how in our poems we're always going back to our first place and the images of our first place, whatever it was, remain fraught with the most meaning for us, or the most potential for us, as writers. . . . Our first place has a different kind of intensity because those were the first trees we ever knew, that was our first river." What does your first place hold for you? What are the images you carry with you, and how do you think it may carry you? What meaning do you give to those images? I think part of what makes something sacred is to give meaning and honor to it. What is it about a particular place that you honor, that you give meaning to?

The fiction writer Carole Maso says about one of her novels, "I composed *Ava* entirely next to water. I doubt it could have been imagined or written in quite the same way without the waves, without the light." She would have written a book elsewhere, but it would not have been the same book. It would not have had the rhythm of the waves and the scent of salt air somewhere in its pages. Consider how where you are right now enters into what you write. Do you think you would write the exact same thing somewhere else?

Does your love of a place affect how well you can write there? When I'm alone in and beside nature, I find there's more space for the sacred to enter my language and my thought process. I'll give in more deeply to the unpredictable, the wild and unkempt. For me, being in the natural world also tends to include not only an openness of physical space, but an openness of time. In contrast to my housed life, outside for days, I have plenty of time to explore this sentence or that, to try out that word twenty-five different times. The poet Brenda Hillman said, "I am in love with California. I can write anywhere in California if I have a chair and a table. Mostly I can write in other places too, but it takes longer."

For poet Philip Levine, it works this way, "I find a spot in the house or the apartment and it becomes the writing place. I don't like a view. I prefer a blank wall. I live four or five months a year in New York City and most of the rest in Fresno. New York City certainly crawls into my writing—*crawls* is the wrong word—charges. The two places are so different, and yet I can write about one while living in the other. I once spent four months in Australia during which I wrote a great deal about the USA; when I got back to Fresno I wrote about Australia." I too find that often it's not till I've left a place that I write best about it. Partly that's just gestation. Partly it's about looking back and longing and distance influencing my viewpoint about experience. But not always. Sometimes being in a place the words seem to come out of that beingness.

Walking Through Valleys, Tunnels, and Walls

Naguib Mahfouz said, "The walk is the important thing. I can sleep on a problem without finding a solution. But when I'm walking, an idea will come to me." Scientists, writers, artists, and other creative people know this to be true. It is an amazing thing. I can't explain it, but I do know it. There is something particular about the rhythm of walking that fosters creative thinking. It enters through our legs, the swing of our arms, faster breath, the heartbeat. And it also has to do with not trying too hard. Don't walk with a pencil in hand! Welcome trust into the picture; the images will stick in your mind and be there when you get back to your desk. Let some air around your writing, let freedom in. We talked a bit about this in Chapter 5, how a change of scene can free you from self-criticism. You become affected and swayed by all you perceive with your senses, including your sense of heart.

Writing in Place

Novelist Mary Gordon writes, "There is a special attachment to a place in which you have written well and happily. There is nothing to remember about the actual experience of writing well, because you are not really there. The joy of it comes from the removal from life, the sense of having been hurled outside the rim of the world. It is only when you come back to the place that has gone on being the same while you were out of it; the desk, the chair, the floor have not rearranged the universe in words. They waited, faithful brides, for your return." Those are places to return to again and again. They afford you the opportunity to dip into the other world and then they welcome you back into the world of the ordinary. I escape to them when I can. In those spots, writing can be viewed as sanctuary. Your desk may be your sanctuary. Begin to take note of the qualities of place that draw your creative spirit in and when you can, go there. What can you do to make your home or your office such a place? Can you turn your chair to a different wall and find yourself where you hadn't been before?

How can you welcome the sacred into the place where you pick up your pen? What might you introduce into your writing ritual that would most call you to feel in connection to God and the Great Spirit? Prayer before work is certainly one way to do it. I know writers who light incense or herbs before they begin to work. Perhaps you want to bring some of nature or another sacred spot into your room, to have with you as you write. When I was in Italy last summer I purchased many postcards of works by Angelico, della Francesco, and others whose pictures of angels, Jesus, and the saints all have a mystical look to them. In Perugia I'd gotten so close to those paintings I could have touched them. I wanted to breathe them in for the look in the angels' eyes that remind me of love, of falling into God when I'm writing.

Nearing the Winter Solstice

Whenever we try to pick out anything by itself we find it hitched to everything else in the universe.

JOHN MUIR

For many years I'd wanted to intimately know a place in the natural world, its paths, how far down this one I could walk till I got tired, the shapes of its trees, their smell and the sound of wind through their branches, to know where the creek fell into a gully. I'd wanted there to be a spot where I could spend hours alone, uninterrupted and relatively unafraid of the potential threat of other people; a place out past cars, cafes, and newspapers; past voices ragged with impatience— my own and others'. I wanted a place that, whether I was there or not, could be inside of me. I wanted someplace to carry in me that might help me hold the bigness of being alive. Rilke writes, "Our task is to stamp this provincial, perishing earth into ourselves so deeply, so painfully and passionately, that its being may rise again, 'invisibly' in us." I dreamed of giving myself to the Earth in some silent way. Could I have seasons of a place and wind-nature in me?

About twelve years ago, I came upon a place where I could be in nature and still sleep in a warm bed, make a cup of tea on an indoor kitchen stove in the morning—a hot springs and hotel, not quite in the middle of nowhere, but a long way down a dirt road, more than twenty miles from town. Not roughing it by any means, but out and away.

You know how it is when you see something from a distance you can only see the generalities of the place? If you were to see Wilbur Hot Springs from a distance, you might think it was generic California landscape. You might think cowboy movies, scrub oak, a few pines, rolling, golden hills. But upon approach and, especially after spending time there, I began to see not *a* place, but *this* place, the ways in which this land is similar to, and different from, others I've spent time in. It took time. The hills are not just golden, they're multicolored, made up of weeds, tall and short grasses, some of which have been flattened by a day's wind or cow hooves. The weeds have names like star thistle and milkweed. There are pale, dry flowers amid those weeds from late summer through early winter, before there's been enough rain to soften the petals until they fade into the grass. The Native Americans of the Colusi, Pomo, and Wintun tribes lived there years ago.

In addition to the land itself, there is the water, hot springs. The Native Americans used the waters of Wilbur for healing and ceremonial purposes for centuries. In the nineteenth century, a medical doctor lived at Wilbur and treated alcoholics using the water. There's actually lithium along with other minerals in it.

It's a place I go to write for several days at a time. If I could afford it, I'd spend longer. No one can reach me there; I leave no mailing address or telephone number. There's no E-mail access; the proprietors of the small, rustic hotel are absurd in their conservation of the only recently installed solar electricity. I'm grateful for that. There are more than fifteen hundred acres to walk through. I like it in winter. It feels even farther away from everything then. It may snow. It may flood. The wind pounds furiously during storms along Bear Valley.

One winter it was particularly cold. On a late afternoon the sky looked foreboding but my feet didn't care, they told me to walk. I must have looked silly, but felt fortunate to be dressed in layer upon layer of sweaters and scarves. Out I went in my good, old boots past the pastures that open from one to the next like rooms in a house without walls. Past the barn more fallen down and crumpled than it had appeared last season. Then under and through the tunnel of trees. Past the huge fig tree no longer with fruit, and to the left up the mountain, along where the manzanita grow so red. I could see my breath in the air but my many sweaters were no longer necessary. At a level spot I stopped to catch my breath, looked down from my climb to one valley and through it to the next and beyond that to another where my vision got blurry and the mountains appeared blue-black. It wasn't forever I was seeing, though it seemed to be what went on ahead.

Once at the crest I began to feel tired and stopped for more view and more breath. It began to hail but only on one side of me. Half of my body was on the side of hail, and the other half was hit with nothing but chill air. I marveled at the coincidence of being in two places at once. Some words suddenly came. A rhythm found me. I turned to walk back down the mountainside, repeating in my mind the phrases that I heard, thought then that I might get back to my room and begin a poem. My step mimicked the pattern of the language. The language mirrored where I was and who I was. Then I had two phrases and said them over and over again, repeated them out loud. Each thing I became aware of, either through my eyes, ears, nose, hands, heart, or mind sketched into language and fell into a rhythm that accompanied what had come before. I had never written a poem this way—words memorized and then more words to remember. There was no hesitation. There was little questioning doubt.

I walked down the mountain. It was raining now and I was wet to the skin. Everything surrounding me had something to say and I had only to listen. I hadn't listened like this before. The words were only my mechanisms. They were what I had to give form to what was being told. It wasn't the mountain's story, not the fallen barn's story. It was mine but not mine alone. It was something between us, between the spirit of a place I knew well enough to fear and not to fear.

When I got down the mountain, back to the tunnel of trees, the rain had almost stopped and there was light like I'd never noticed before. It was touching the leaves and the branches, the barbed-wire fences. The sky had some light, though I'm not completely sure it came from there. The creek had light moving through its water. So the light went into the poem too. And it was nearly Christmas so that got in there. I think my surprise is in the poem too. I'll leave it here for you to see if you think so.

Nearing the Winter Solstice

Along the ridge top, after a hard climb, I walked
to just where the rainstorm began, stood for a while
with one foot on either side, straddling
the boundary of weather, proving, that in fact,
you can be in two places at the same time.

In what light remained, I watched nearby
and toward the mountains so far away
they became black wings, how the light held
what it touched in radiance, so that everything
became all that it could be, all that it was
on the best of days. The trunk of the craggy
manzanita became more certainly red than I had
ever seen before. It seemed to call out, like a bell,
to whomever was listening, saying, I am this
manzanita tree. And the green blades of grass,
each one, tilting down then rising up, seemed to say,
I am this grass, shiny and bright. The enormous wind
that pushed into my ears, made everything move.
Light, like in the paintings of Baby Jesus,
how his face holds it so completely he gives it away,
enlivening everything that passes.

Quickly, now that the rain had become hail,
the thick clouds gathering, I walked back down
the ridge, past the cows grazing homeward,
past the cold spring rushing, past the fallen barn
musty and hollow, past the dampening fields
spread out in all directions, past everything familiar,
which until this light, I had never seen before.

PAUSING AT THE WELL
Silence and Solitude

Between breaths there is a slight pause, between the inhale and the exhale and especially between the exhale and the next inhale. Most of the time it's brief as a comma. A place of silence, where emptiness exists between two points, the pouring out and filling up. In this tiny no-man's-land we may be found alone doing nothing every day in the midst of all we do. It's a moment of nothing between two somethings.

If you begin to imagine solitude from there, aloneness is a brief pause. Could you just be there in that tiniest of spaces, alone in nothing? Consider the unfilled full. Imagine a hammock between the two places as suspended securely and swinging slightly. What's there in the in-between? Is it deep or shallow, dark or light, warm or cold, that place between two breaths? Aloneness doesn't have to be bigger than we are. It can be a small space in which we place ourselves for its teaching, for the rest of a pause, to give pause, to take that momentary space.

John Ciardi said, "The ideal poem is a stirring awake of words in a haunted silence. It is not an assertion but a being, a harkening to being, and a way of being." For the writer silence and solitude are sustenance. Words come out of it. Creative work is preceded and followed by silence. Fill your life with perpetual sound and action and company, and you may find your words avoiding you. In silence a writer mulls and culls. May Sarton said, "Silence was the food I was after, silence and the country itself—trees, meadows, hills, the open sky." As writing can be a place, so can silence.

Where do you go for silence and solitude? To the woods? To the barn? To your empty office on a Saturday night? What do you find waiting for you there? I find that for silence and solitude to have meaning in my life and practice, what's most important isn't the amount of it, it's the commitment to having it and getting it on a regular basis. I have no children; it makes finding silence easier than for those with kids at home, I know. My student Linda has a demanding job, running a martial arts school. She's married and the mother of a young boy. Linda tells me that after she drops Nathan off for school she drives to the beach and sits and writes most mornings for fifteen minutes. "These days," she says, "that's just not enough."

The Quiet

During the nights of the past month I've been sleeping only in fits and starts. I'm coming up at finishing writing this book and I can't shut it off, no matter what I do. Not even when I sleep. After tossing and turning for a while I generally get up, jealous of Michael who is asleep most nights even before his head hits the pillow. Without turning a light on, I go out to the living room, wrap myself in a blanket, and sit on the couch. It's when I begin consciously breathing that I realize how shallow my breath had been. Hating insomnia, knowing how miserable I'll be come morning, I pray. I imagine holding the poet within in my arms and try listening to her. "I want to be asleep," she tells me. "Me, too," I reply. Nothing to argue about here. After a while I tend to begin writing, but not at my computer or with paper and pencil. I stay on the couch and I work the words back and forth, in and out. I continue on with whatever chapter I was writing during the day. Or I begin revising previous chapters. Then I go back to moaning (quietly) about my lack of sleep and how horribly tired I'll feel come morning.

The other day I realized that I like this time. I don't like the anxiety. But I do like the largeness of silence the midnight hours give me; I can't get them at any other time of day. It feels like an odd privilege, though frankly, I'd rather be sleeping. Apparently part of me, a rather dominant part, disagrees. Silence late at night is shrouded; it's enclosed time and space, unalterable. No one will want anything of me now. The phone won't ring. This silence is protecting me. It's not protecting me from sleep; it's providing me with uncluttered time to be, to breathe, to meditate, to think, and to write. During those late-night times, my mind moves more softly when I focus it on the book because I don't feel bound by anything. There's no way I'm going to get up and turn a light and the computer on. I'm just going to be here awake and within whatever approaches.

Until just recently I'd feel afraid when I'd be up at night and I still get angry sometimes, but not as often. Instead of flinging myself into the anger, I pray, and when I pray in the silence, I get soft inside and kinder. The silence moves into greater silence and it does seem as though I'm protected by it. There are times when silence may not be what we want, but if it's what we've got, then the choice is to embrace it or fight it. I'm learning to be held by the bigness of late-night silence. And then, amazingly, I drift to sleep.

You may find yourself in need of silence—perhaps not midnight silence but a quietude that can be found during daylight hours. It may mean you write out of that silence, or it may mean you keep the quiet like a pact, until you know it's time for words or something else that you pray for. Silence is to the writer like air. It keeps us alive and writing.

Interruptions in the Silence

You're writing. It's quiet when the phone rings, but you think, so what's a little interruption, and pick up the receiver. A crackly sound and muffled voices in the background and you know either it's telephone sales or an international call. An unfamiliar voice says, "Is this so-and-so?" You reply, "No, no you may not speak to him." You hang up the phone in relief. But an interruption has gotten under your skin, having to use the voice when it was silently occupied before. Next time, unplug yourself from distractions. The distractions generated by your own mind will be more than enough.

Friday was a spirit-word day. I was writing smooth and with certainty. The falseness came in when I tried to pretend that it was OK with me that by afternoon our house would be descended upon by a significant portion of Michael's family, whom I dearly love. His immediate family is large enough to make a large, fun, and boisterous party. I like a loud party.

The problem is that in writing this book I need solitude and silence. And to not consider others' needs and desires is difficult in theory and even more difficult in practice. Having company feels like getting pulled off the path. And I've got to work hard enough inside myself—practically and spiritually—to stay on it, that external interference is too much. Am I being selfish? Does this need of mine make me a snob? Can I even dare to call it a need? But I don't know what else to call it when everything I've got goes onto the page. These days I want acres of silence and solitude.

First I had to make the path. And there were a lot of trees, an assortment of debris, including imaginary junk cars, dump loads of torn Kleenex, and years of fear and hesitation to move before I could get to anything resembling soft and solid ground. But I'm here now. Every day I give myself to the path and the walking, but I can't seem to give myself to interruptions of the large-group-of-people kind. I can look like I give myself to them. I can be gracious and elegant. But I'm a tiger inside who wants her four paws on the path.

It's sort of like having a lot of people around fills my heart space and my head space with them instead of with this book. There may be times for you too, when you're writing and want to give that precedence. I don't think you're being selfish. I think it means you're being a writer. Balancing the rest of life with writing, spiritually or otherwise, is an act requiring humor, tenderness, and patience toward yourself and others.

For the Notebook 1

CREATING A WRITING MANDALA

Mandalas are circular designs that radiate out from a center point like the sun. The Sanskrit word *mandala* means circle. Images of mandalas exist throughout nature—melons, pomegranates, eyes, shells, snowflakes, stars. Labyrinths are mandalas that one walks through as a meditation practice. A maze is another kind of mandala. Jung referred to them as, "a blueprint of some aspect of creation." They possess symbols of the universe and its energy.

For ages, mandalas have been a part of many spiritual traditions, including Native American, Tibetan, and Indian. They have been used in psychology to support healing work. In the Tibetan tradition, all religious works of art are collectively referred to as support. Mandalas are "mind supports," representations of the spiritual embodiment of the Buddha. The Tibetan term for them is *dkyil khor*, which translates as "center-circumference." It describes both the geometric structure and the ritual meaning of mandalas. The essence, the heart of the Buddha, exists at the center, and the circumference is the place of grasping the essence.

Mandalas reflect on the harmony of our spiritual selves. My friend Wendy, who uses mandala creation in her healing work with cancer patients, says that, "A mandala is a picture that tells the whole story. Both creating and viewing them brings one a sense of wholeness." To recognize and foster this harmony, you might like to make your own mandala, symbolizing the place that writing holds in your life, or the place you would like it to and how silence, solitude, and sacred place enter your work. Can the mandala itself be a sacred place?

In Judith Cornell's book *Mandalas*, she presents them on black paper. I like the idea of color coming out of darkness, and it works as a symbol for writing, words coming from no words. Get yourself some large paper so you can spread out and physically enter your writing place. Chalk pastels—soft and hard—are an excellent medium to work with; you can create hard edges or smooth ones and blend color and form.

The small circle at the middle of a mandala is said to represent the pure mind or one's essence. What is at the center of your desire to write? What's the pure, heartful motivation? What color or image could you draw to inhabit that space? You might begin there. Or perhaps, for you, the radiating energy is what comes first. How does writing contain you? And what holds your writing in place?

Keep in mind as you draw that the idea is what's known as "process art." The process of making, not the product, is primary. You may find your direction changing as you go. That's another reason I like working in pastels. They can take my change of heart and let me layer color and form over color and form with no resistance, creating a melding of both. The other thing to remember is there's another piece of paper. (Make sure you've got more than one!) So if what you draw first doesn't get you all the way there, you can keep going.

You may make something that holds for you both that home place within that we talked about in Chapter 1, as well as the place for your writing. Perhaps they are one and the same. Your mandala may be something you want to fold and tuck into your journal or hang on your wall. It will serve as a reminder that within your depth, there exists a place for your words.

In addition to making mandalas for individual practice, a writers' group might embark on the creation of a group mandala. For Tibetan monks, the collaboration process of making mandalas is more valuable than their originality. As a group, begin with a large sheet of paper or fabric spread out on the floor. You might have a focus for your creation, such as creating an image of the group, or you might discover the form and focus as you go. You may choose to work simultaneously or approach the mandala one at a time. After making the mandala, you might write a group piece as well as individual pieces about the work. What's there? What moves? How do the colors speak to you? What does the center say? What's the message of the outer rays?

As an individual project the process of making the mandala might take you one hour or several. I find that once I begin, I want to keep going, don't want to be hemmed in by time constraints. It's ideal to give yourself an entire afternoon or evening. You may wish to return to the piece for writing. And you may be inspired to write from and to the mandala more than once.

The Tibetans and Navajos are known for their mandalas made of sand, temporary structures built of impermanent material. Upon completion, the Tibetans deliberately destroy the mandalas, sweeping the sand into a nearby stream or river. If you've made your mandala out of paper and you wish to destroy it, you might burn the piece. But be with it first. Write from it and to it. Notice how even after the object is gone from the physical world the impressions it leaves remain with you.

For the Notebook 2

CONVERSATIONS IN THE NATURAL WORLD

Speak to the earth and it shall answer thee, ask the beasts and they shall teach thee and the birds of the air and they shall tell thee and the fish shall tell thee.

DHUODA, *Handbook for William*

Take your notebook outside. Find a good spot to sit down—a boulder, a log, a grassy meadow—and write. You might begin with the smallest thing you see. Or the largest. The tiniest sound, the barely audible one, then the loudest. Take all the ways you have of knowing the world with you and invite them into the process of writing. How do you know the sacred? How do you know the Earth?

A process I've found both delightful and inspirational is to ask questions of my surroundings and write what I hear, as though to engage in a call and response. Sky, where did you get your blue? Ocean, what depth do you have? What's the hungriest thing in the sea? Where's the darkest place in a tree? Who are you, bird, all by yourself and at such a height? Snake, where are you traveling? To ask implies listening. Out in the natural world is the finest place I know of to listen for God. It requires I open my eyes, my ears, my heart.

For this exercise, a good amount of time is preferable. Take a long walk and bring your notebook along. Try to get to someplace unfamiliar and see what's there. The backyard will do just fine as well. The sun shines there as it does on any open meadow.

For the Notebook 3

YOUR ANIMAL NATURE

If you were to consider yourself an animal, what animal would it be? This is a favorite activity of mine from childhood. I would be a lion, hawk, or house cat and found it easy to slip into my perception of that animal. What animal is your poet within or the internal critic? What habitat do they live in? What does the growl or the sense of flight have to say? What's the movement of a lizard through the dust? Years ago I did work with a therapist to discover the animal presences at various chakras, or energy points, in my body. The male lion with an enormous mane has stayed with me. Whenever I am afraid, I call on his fierceness to save me. And it does. What is your wildness and where does it dwell?

Close your eyes and sit quietly till the image of an animal emerges. Notice how it moves and sounds, the texture of its fur. What message does it have for you? Does this animal align you with God and the Great Spirit? Does it bring you nearer your own authentic nature? You might choose to draw or paint the animal first and then find words to accompany the picture. Give yourself an hour or so of unhampered time and see how many pages come out of it.

EPILOGUE

Journeys by Heart

For a while now the butcher at my local grocery store and I have been greeting each other in Spanish, a word or two, that's it. Recently Teo asked if I speak Spanish. I told him, "Only a very little." "Then I will teach you," he said with certainty. He's a native speaker, and his Spanish is lilting and fast. Mine is raggedy and slow. My previous Spanish teachers have all been the children whose classrooms I've worked in. I can speak fairly well, in an elementary way, about poetry. *Una poema es una dibuja hecho de palabras.* "A poem is a picture made of words," I tell my young students. I like attempting conversations in Spanish with Teo. I appreciate his correcting me.

The other day when I came in to get food for dinner, Teo asked me how I was. "I'm tired," I answered. "Me too," he said, and asked the cause of my tiredness. I was up against the limits of my Spanish there, and did my best to explain that I was editing a manuscript. Teo understood me just fine. "You're a writer!" he exclaimed. "I'm going to write a book someday," he said seriously but with a glint of slyness in his eye. I told him I thought that would be a great idea. "It will be the history of my life. But, alas, it will be an ugly story." "Why ugly? Have you had an ugly life?" "Well, it's a long story. And yours," he asked, "how is it?" "I wouldn't call it ugly. It's easy and it's hard; hard between my ears mostly. These days," I went on, "I'm a little broke, but I do have love." I'm sure I conveyed the gist of what I was trying

to say. "Ah, love is the ultimate!" he said, looking at me doubtfully.
Someday I hope to read Teo's story, to see just how he'd take language and make something of it that I could hold in my hands.

Thumbing through a recent *New Yorker*, I came upon a poem by
John Hollander tucked neatly between the text of a story and an
advertisement. It's about the things we know by heart, in the order
they come to us when we stop to remember. He says that songs are
the first to come to mind, then poems, and those are followed by
night's sounds—a train's whistle, swallows on a summer evening. In
"By Heart," Hollander writes about music in our memory: "We play
by ear, but learn the words by heart. . . ."

I hope *Writing and the Spiritual Life* supports you on your journey
through the things you know by heart, and that you continue to make
a space in your life for telling stories. Along your writing journey—
through its static moments and its startling ones, and all that's in
between—may you hold your ground, open-eyed, a creator and witness to life's details and complexities, alert to the marvelous errors and
the outrageous crimes. Your art will make a path for you to follow and
along the way the things you know by heart will broaden and increase.
Making art out of life will smooth and shorten the distance between
you and your God.

Suggested Reading

The Divine Comedy, by Dante Alighieri. The John Ciardi Translation. New York, London: W. W. Norton, 1970.

The Poetics of Reverie: Childhood, Language, and the Cosmos, by Gaston Bachelard. Boston: Beacon Press, 1971.

The Selected Poetry of Yehuda Amichai, edited and translated by Chana Bloch and Stephen Mitchell. Berkeley: University of California Press, 1996.

The Myth of the Goddess: Evolution of an Image, by Anne Baring and Jules Cashford. New York: Viking Books, 1991.

Crossing to Avalon: A Woman's Midlife Pilgrimage, by Jean Shinoda Bolen. San Francisco: HarperSan Francisco, 1995.

Where We Stand: Women Poets on Literary Tradition, edited by Sharon Bryan. New York: W. W. Norton, 1993.

The Sacred Place: Witnessing the Holy in the Physical World, edited by Scott Cairns and W. Scott Olsen. Salt Lake City: University of Utah Press, 1996.

Joseph Campbell: An Open Life: Joseph Campbell in Conversation with Michael Toms, by Joseph Campbell, Michael Toms, and Dennis Biggs (eds.). New York: HarperCollins, 1990.

Ciardi Himself: Fifteen Essays in the Reading, Writing, and Teaching of Poetry, by John Ciardi. Fayetteville, London: University of Arkansas Press, 1989.

The Flashboat: Poems Collected and Reclaimed, by Jane Cooper. New York, London: W. W. Norton, 2000.

The Hero's Journey: Joseph Campbell on His Life and Work, edited by Phil Couineau. Boston: Element Books, 1999.

Homo Aestheticus: Where Art Comes from and Why, by Ellen Dissanayake. Seattle: University of Washington Press, 1995.

Be Careful What You Pray for . . . You Just Might Get It, by Larry Dossey. New York: HarperCollins, 1998.

Meditations from a Moveable Chair, by Andre Dubus. New York: Vintage Books, 1999.

Creation Myths, by Marie-Louise von Franz. Boston: Shambhala Press, 1995.

Being Bodies: Buddhist Women on the Paradox of Embodiment, edited by Lenore Friedman and Susan Moon. Boston: Shambhala Press, 1997.

Reading Rilke: Reflections on the Problems of Translation, by William H. Gass. New York: Alfred A. Knopf, Inc., 1999.

Seeing Through Places: Reflections on Geography and Identity, by Mary Gordon. New York: Scribner, 2000.

Sacraments of Desire, by Linda Gregg. Saint Paul, MN: Graywolf Press, 1991.

Things and Flesh, by Linda Gregg. Saint Paul, MN: Graywolf Press, 1999.

Writing a Woman's Life, by Carolyn Heilbrun. New York: W. W. Norton, 1989.

Room to Fly: A Transcultural Memoir, by Padma Hejmadi. Berkeley: University of California Press, 1999.

A Blue Fire: Selected Writings, by James Hillman (edited by Thomas Moore). New York: HarperPerennial, 1991.

The Gift: Imagination and the Erotic Life of Property, by Lewis Hyde. New York: Vintage Books Edition, Random House, Inc., 1983.

The Hidden Writer: Diaries and the Creative Life, by Alexandra Johnson. New York: Doubleday, 1998.

The Complete Poems of Emily Dickinson, edited by Thomas H. Johnson. Boston: Little, Brown. 1976.

A Hundred White Daffodils, by Jane Kenyon. Port Townsend, WA: Copper Canyon Press, 1999.

The Lion, the Witch and the Wardrobe, by C. S. Lewis. New York: Harper-Collins, 1950.

The Golden Key, by George MacDonald. New York: Farrar, Straus & Giroux, 1992.

Ava, by Carole Maso. Normal, IL: Dalkey Archive Press, 1995.

A Roadside Dog, by Czeslaw Milosz. New York: Farrar, Straus & Giroux, 1999.

Care of the Soul: A Guide for Cultivating Depth and Sacredness in Everyday Life, by Thomas Moore. New York: HarperCollins, 1992.

Beloved, by Toni Morrison. New York: Alfred A. Knopf, Inc., 1998.

Toni Morrison: Lecture and Speech of Acceptance, upon the Award of the Nobel Prize for Literature, Delivered in Stockholm on the Seventh of December. New York: Alfred A. Knopf, Inc., 1994.

Merleau-Ponty: Interiority and Exteriority, Psychic Life and the World, edited by Dorothea Orlkowski and James Morley. Albany, NY: State University Press, 1999.

The Inferno of Dante: A New Verse Translation, bilingual edition, by Robert Pinsky. New York: Farrar, Straus & Giroux, 1995.

Letters to a Young Poet, by Rainer Maria Rilke (translated by Stephen Mitchell). New York: Random House, 1987.

The Collected Poems of Theodore Roethke, by Theodore Roethke. New York: Anchor Books/Doubleday, 1975.

On Women Turning Seventy, by Cathleen Rountree. San Francisco: Jossey-Bass, 1999.

Walking on Alligators: A Book of Meditations for Writers, by Susan Shaughnessy. San Francisco: HarperSanFrancisco, 1993.

Conversations with Maxine Hong Kingston, edited by Paul Skenazy and Tera Martin. Jackson: University Press of Mississippi, 1998.

Ariadne's Clue: A Guide to the Symbols of Humankind, by Anthony Stevens. Princeton, CT: Princeton University Press, 1999.

Storming Heaven's Gate: Spiritual Writings by Women, edited by Amber C. Sumrall and Patrice Vecchione. New York: Plume/Penguin Putnam, 1997.

The Spiritual Quest: Transcendence in Myth, Religion, and Science, by Robert M. Torrance. Berkeley: University of California Press, 1994.

CREDITS